Teamwork from Start to Finish:
10 Steps to Results!

Teamwork from Start to Finish

10 Steps to Results

Fran Rees

Pfeiffer

An Imprint of Jossey-Bass Inc., Publishers

Copyright © 1997 by Pfeiffer, An Imprint of Jossey-Bass Inc., Publishers

ISBN: 0–7879–1061–9

Library of Congress Cataloging-in-Publication Data

Rees, Fran.
    Teamwork from start to finish : 10 steps to results / Fran Rees.
        p.   cm.
    Includes bibliographical references and index.
    ISBN 0–7879–1061–9
    1. Work groups. I. Title.
    HD66.R3943   1997
    658.4'2—dc21   97–4606
                                                                                       CIP

Printed in the United States of America

Published by

An Imprint of Jossey-Bass Inc., Publishers
350 Sansome Street, 5th Floor
San Francisco, California 94104–1342
(415) 433–1740; Fax (415) 433–0499
Pfeiffer (800) 274–4434; Fax (800) 569–0443

Visit our website at: http://www.pfeiffer.com

Outside of the United States, Pfeiffer products can be purchased from the following Simon & Schuster International Offices:

Prentice Hall Canada
PTR Division
1870 Birchmount Road
Scarborough, Ontario M1P 2J7
Canada
(800) 567–3800; Fax (800) 263–7733

Simon & Schuster (Asia) Pte Ltd
317 Alexandra Road
#04–01 IKEA Building
Singapore 159965
Asia
65 476 4688; Fax 65 378 0370

Prentice Hall
Campus 400
Maylands Avenue
Hemel Hempstead
Hertfordshire HP2 7EZ
United Kingdom
44(0) 1442 881891; Fax 44(0) 1442 882288

Prentice Hall Professional
Locked Bag 531
Frenchs Forest PO NSW 2068
Australia
61 2 9907 5693; Fax 61 2 9905 7934

Prentice Hall/Pfeiffer
P.O. Box 1636
Randburg 2125
South Africa
27 11 781 0780; Fax 27 11 781 0781

Printing   10   9   8   7   6   5   4   3   2   1

This book is printed on acid-free, recycled stock that meets or exceeds the minimum GPO and EPA requirements for recycled paper.

Dedication

This book is dedicated to the teams and individuals who helped me write this book:

- To the work teams I have worked with over the years and the leaders in organizations who support teams.
- To the consulting clients who asked me to facilitate and train teams in their organizations.
- To the publishing team at Pfeiffer who evaluated, edited, and produced the book.
- And to the all-important "home team": David, my husband, who contributed to numerous conversations about the book and unfailingly supported the process; and Lauren, my twelve-year-old daughter, for her consideration and understanding on those days I was glued to the computer.

You are all part of the synergy that made this book happen. A resounding and heartfelt Thank You!

Table of Contents

Phase I: Getting Organized

Step Three: Establish Ground Rules   86

Phase II: Producing   97

Step Four: Plan the Work   99

Introduction

Being a professional today requires an understanding of teamwork, and successful experience as a team member or team leader enhances your value to an employer. Managers, supervisors, and employees in many organizations are now routinely expected to lead or work on teams to increase productivity, improve quality, and achieve high levels of customer satisfaction. In many organizations today, teamwork has become a critical avenue for getting things done.

The realization of the value of teamwork has raced ahead of our understanding of what it takes to achieve results through teams. Much has been talked of, written about, and developed in relation to teams. Authors have focused on the importance of teams, leading teams, the benefits of teams, building team spirit, and transitioning to teams. Yet, little has been done to help teams approach teamwork as a step-by-step journey with a clear destination. Teams can easily get derailed, lose focus, or become bogged down.

Over the years, I have worked as a consultant with teams in all kinds of organizations (service industry, computer companies, government, healthcare, education, and police work). In this work, I have found that a team needs some kind of a blueprint to carry it along. Whether the team is an ongoing, intact work team, or a team on special assignment, it faces a beginning, middle, and end, or crossroads, in its work as a team.

When the team follows a step-by-step procedure to get its work done, the team members are much less apt to founder, get confused, or give up. Instead, the team has a sense of control over its own destiny, and team members can see a shape to their collaborative efforts. The team can learn to chart its own course, evaluate its progress, and self-correct.

The more a team controls *how* it gets the work done, the quicker it becomes a well-functioning unit. Many teams do not know how to get work done. Frequently, teams are created and challenged to work as a unit, but even when the team members are ready to work, they are not clear about what steps to take and when to take them. As a result, some teams get off to a poor start and never really function well as a unit. For example, without a blueprint, the "doers" on the team who are ready to implement ideas and plans immediately must wait while the "analyzers" debate and discuss the purpose or goals of the team before anyone can take action. Team members in the middle of the spectrum try to appease the "doers" and the "analyzers," so the more dominant group does not take over and make all the decisions.

Ideally, there should be a balance of analysis and action within the team. Indeed, the two characteristics will help a team work through its goals. The step-by-step approach presented in this book allows for both analyzing and doing by the team members in order to get results as a team. When the steps are followed, the team is more likely to be productive.

The actual work of a team has an understandable flow. The development of the team—how it grows over time from a novice team into a more mature, fully functioning team—also has a beginning, a middle, and an end. Both the work the team does and the growth of the team must be attended to by the members. This book is an outgrowth of this need—how to organize and move forward as a team, step by step.

In order for teams to work, they must function well in two dimensions: getting the *work* done (which is a relatively linear process) and building and maintaining the *spirit and momentum* of the team (which is a cyclical, dynamic, and non-linear process). Teams cannot ignore either dimension. Indeed, team results are achieved only if both dimensions are taken care of. The ten steps presented in this book help the team progress in both dimensions.

Teamwork is simply a group of people working together as a unit. It is not some mystical process or some magical chemical mixture of people that may take or not. Teamwork may be a lot of hard work, but it is not mystical. Most teams that follow certain guidelines and present a concentrated effort to function as a productive and unified team will be successful.

The purpose of this book is to help organizations create effective teams. By taking the step-by-step approach outlined in this book, an organization's team will have a better chance of working cohesively and achieving desired results.

Working together is the key to successful organizations. Teamwork, in the context of high-performing and empowered teams, is one of our most advanced methods of working together today. Teamwork is a challenging, and sometimes ticklish, process of managing people and work in a group setting. To make things a bit more difficult, teamwork usually happens within the changing and complex environments of organizations and the marketplace. It makes sense that successful teamwork will require order, planning, patience, persistence, and ongoing adjustments. A successful team requires people who are coached and trained to work in teams, who understand the essential steps to achieving results as a team, and who are willing to work at building and maintaining the team.

How to Use This Book

This book will guide your team through ten major steps to help produce desired results. The first half of the book discusses the ten steps so your team can understand each one. The second half of the book consists of practical lessons in teamwork. These lessons represent important ideas and processes that support the ten steps in teamwork. Your team will certainly stumble along if it does not apply basic principles of good teamwork found in the lessons, such as holding productive team meetings and making decisions through consensus.

Because team members cannot learn or do everything at once, they should not try to learn all the lessons at one time. Instead, the team members should review one or two lessons at a time as they proceed through the steps. The members should use the practical lessons found in the book as the team needs them and when it needs them. They are there for training, guidance, review, and reference.

There are other lessons your team will need to learn, and the team should appoint a member to build a reference library of materials, such as those listed in the bibliography at the end of this book. These materials will come in handy when the team faces its unique issues and situations. Also, your team should not overlook the most valuable resource that lies in the experience of other teams. Talk to other team members and leaders and find out how other successful teams have solved their problems. Your team should find out what made other teams fail or give up; this will help members evaluate themselves as a team (Step Six). This will be one of your team's greatest resources: the ability to give yourself constructive feedback and make corrections in how you work as a team. All of these resources will help your team steer around the roadblocks and avoid the inevitable pitfalls of teamwork.

This book focuses on guiding a new team: helping it get started, move forward, achieve goals, and finish its work. However, the book is also useful for teams already in existence and for ongoing teams. The same steps apply. If your team is already functioning as a team, use the book to help you determine where you are, review your work as a team, correct your course, and move on. For example, if you don't have a clear team charter, stop and review what you are doing as a team, where you are going, and write your charter. A charter will give your team energy and focus. If it is an ongoing team, completing Step Ten (Move On) will refocus your team and give it new direction. Whether your team is a new one with inexperienced team members, a new team of experienced team members, or a team that has been working together for some time, this book will give you guidance in achieving results as a work unit.

The principles of teamwork outlined here apply to all types of teams: manufacturing teams, service teams, staff teams, community teams, executive teams, cross-functional project teams, implementation teams, and many others. Try to follow the ten steps outlined in this book. You may have to change some of the questions and terminology so that the steps will work in your organization. You can incorporate the practical lessons in teamwork along the way. If necessary, adapt these guidelines to what your team needs.

As your team works through the steps, it should keep in mind the dual aspect of teamwork: getting the work done (achieving the goals) and building a cohesive unit (getting along well as team members). Hopefully, your team will weather the normal ups and downs of teamwork while being productive and creating a sense of camaraderie that leaves team members believing that they can accomplish their goal because they are a team.

When your team faces problems or loses momentum, stop and ask the following questions:

- What step is our team on in the journey?
- Has the team advanced ahead before completing a previous step, or regressed by rehashing a step already completed?
- Are we stuck on one step because of a disagreement?
- What processes are we overlooking that could help us proceed?
- Are we paying attention to how we operate as a team?
- What are we ignoring that is causing disharmony in the team?
- What can we do to be more productive as a team?

Once you find the problem as a team, solve it as a team and do what is necessary to get back on track.

How to Assess the Need for a Team

A team is not always the most effective or efficient way to get work done. To determine whether a team is the best option, a manager, a team leader, or the team members will need to do the following:

1. Describe the work to be done.
2. Determine whether a team is the most effective way to get the work done.
3. Decide what type of team is needed and how the team will work within the organization.
4. Select team members.

Describe the Work to Be Done

Whoever assesses the need for a team should think of the work in terms of output. What will be the result of this work? Will a problem be solved, a decision made, a product produced, a service rendered, a process improved, a new system set up, or a project completed? Given the expected end result, what is the scope and type of work that needs to be done?

Are there any other organizational goals the work is going to support? For example, is the work expected to change the organization's culture, system, or procedures? Are there others in the organization with a similar mission, or will this work pioneer a new effort? Is it necessary to change the way the organization or a particular group has been working together? In many cases, teams are formed to improve the quality of work being done by a work group that hasn't been functioning as a team. In these cases, a team is formed to improve the quality, productivity, and effectiveness of an existing work group.

Determine Whether a Team Is Needed

Those assessing the need for a team must think about why a team might be needed to perform particular work. For example, can the work be done more effectively by an individual? Other questions to consider are, What added value to the end result will a team provide? Is there already a team, a work group, a task force, or a committee in existence that could do the work?

Following are some guidelines for determining whether a team is needed. An organization should consider using a team if the work requires one or more of the following:

- A variety of skills, experiences, judgments, and abilities
- Ideas and feedback from different units in, or related to, the organization
- Interdependence (i.e., various activities within the scope of the work are closely dependent and connected to one another)
- Several people or positions all work toward the same goal
- Buy-in and cooperation from several people or groups to be successful
- Innovation and synergy
- Relatively quick assembly, deployment, and disbanding of people, as opposed to setting up more permanent structures and processes

- Organization-wide representation, decision making, and buy-in
- Mutual and shared, versus individual, accountability and ownership for the work done

Determine What Type of Team Is Needed

Once the purpose and nature of the team has been determined, the next step—before forming the team—is for the manager or team members to determine what type of team is needed to meet the organization's purpose. Is the team going to be an ongoing work team that stays together indefinitely to produce a product or deliver a service? Or is the team going to be a project team that will disband after the project is complete? Will the team come together for a brief period to make a recommendation or decision, or will the team stay together for several months or even years? Following are some descriptions of teams. If a team is needed, determine which description best describes how the team fits into the organization.

Intact Work Team   An intact work team is usually an operational, ongoing work team that reports to a manager or supervisor. The direct supervisor may be assigned the role of team leader, or someone else in the team may fill this role. Intact work teams are given varying degrees of responsibility and authority. A truly self-directed work team is usually made responsible for a whole product, process, service, or clearly defined segment of work. The team plans, performs, manages, and corrects its own work. In experienced teams, the team members may choose and replace their team members and the team leader, and provide input to performance reviews and merit increases of team members. Some teams may be given limited autonomy. Teams with shared authority for their work are called *semi-autonomous work teams*. These teams, although responsible for a whole product, process, service, or a clearly defined segment of work, must work in conjunction with management to plan, perform, manage, and correct their own work. Most intact teams in organizations today are semi-autonomous.

Project Team A project team is made up of selected individuals (sometimes from different work groups or functions) who work on a specific assignment in addition to their regular jobs. In some cases, team members are assigned to the project full time and when the project is completed, they are reassigned to another team or job. Indeed, in the rapidly changing workplace, there are fewer and fewer defined jobs and more and more project-oriented assignments. Other names for project teams are cross-functional team, task force, and problem-solving team.

After determining the type of team needed for the project, the next question to address is how will the team link to what is going on in the organization. Determine what communication channels or reporting structures make sense for this team, given its purpose. Will the team simply fit into the existing organization structure and report to a supervisor or manager, who may now be called a team leader? Operational teams and intact work teams usually report to team leaders. Will the team operate parallel to the organization structure and report into the organization in a non-traditional way? Will the team be under close supervision or will it be self-directing and autonomous? Will the team have a leader and/or sponsor (sometimes called a mentor) that links the team to the organization and guides or coaches the team?

If the team will be self-directing, how much autonomy will the team have? The team members should know if they will have the authority to carry out the team's decisions or if they will be expected to function within traditional constraints, such as getting management's approval on its decisions. The team members will need to know what constraints will be put on the team. Management should remember that one of the key reasons for starting a team is to move the decision making and problem solving to the people who have firsthand knowledge of the situation or process. In an excellent resource book for teams, *The Team Handbook: How to Use Teams to Improve Quality*, Peter R. Scholtes says:

> In most organizations, decisions are made two or three hierarchical levels above where they should be made. Projects provide an

opportunity to empower groups at the lower levels, groups that normally include operators of the process, with authority to decide on changes.[1]

The manager or project leader should keep this in mind when deciding how much autonomy the team should have. If the team is made up of "experts" needed to solve the problem and a good representation of "implementers" who will carry out the team's efforts, then the team should be given the authority needed to make decisions and implement them. If most of the team's decisions must be approved by higher levels of management, the morale and the effort of the team members will be undermined. This could also negatively affect productivity.

Many teams have worked hard to solve a problem or arrive at a decision only to be countered or disapproved by someone higher up in the organization. These team members were less than enthusiastic when assigned to another team.

Determine Who Will Support the Team and How

The team will need to know if it will be sponsored by a manager and what type of support it will have within the organization. For example, the team will need to know who will fund it and provide key organizational information. The team should also know who will be responsible for the performance and results of the team. If the team is to move toward being self-managed, how will the team get there? What type of leadership, funding, training, and other support will the team need?

Take Initiative to Request a Team

Many organizations today are experimenting with getting things done through teamwork. Even if you believe that you do not have

---

[1] From *The Team Handbook: How to Use Teams to Improve Quality* by Peter R. Scholtes, (Madison: Joiner Associates, 1988). Used by permission.

the authority to recommend the creation of a team, do not let that stop you from recommending it to someone who can. Use the checklist and the justification worksheet at the end of this chapter to determine if a team is needed. The worksheet will help you gather information to show your manager or your organization how it can benefit from using a team to achieve a particular result. You may be surprised at the positive response. There have been several instances where management was excited when employees took the initiative to identify a need for a team. Sometimes employees are afraid to speak up and make suggestions because their organizations' cultures did not welcome proactive behavior. Don't wait for management to tell you there is a problem or a decision or an improvement needed. Present your suggestion thoroughly, answer questions in a straightforward way, and ask management whether they will support the idea.

If management rejects your suggestion, don't give up. Use this as an opportunity to learn more about your management and your organization. Ask your manager or the management group how you could have presented the idea differently, or what problems they have with the idea. Try to listen without getting defensive. Repeat what the manager or the group told you to clarify your understanding. In most cases, management will appreciate your taking professional initiative to help your organization be successful.

Note: When presenting a suggestion, avoid insinuating poor performance on anyone else's part, or suggesting to solve a problem someone else is already working on. Speak with others and get good information and opinions before making a formal suggestion to start a team.

Checklist for Identifying the Need for a Team

Identify the work that needs to be done:

___ A problem solved

___ A decision made

___ A product produced

___ A service rendered

___ A process improved

___ A plan made and implemented

___ A new system set up

___ A project completed

___ Other:

___ Briefly describe the work that needs to be done.

___ Estimate the scope and length of the work to be done (i.e., the time frame, the number of people needed, the money needed).

___ List other organizational goals this work supports (e.g., production and/or quality goals, cultural change, improved market share).

___ Determine whether the work to be done ties to work already being done in the organization or if this is a pioneer effort.

___ Determine whether a team is the most effective way to get the work done.

   ___ A variety of skills, experiences, judgments, and abilities

   ___ Ideas and feedback from different units in, or related to, the organization

   ___ Interdependence (i.e., various activities within the scope of the work are closely dependent and connected to one another)

   ___ Several people or positions all work toward the same goal

__ Buy-in and cooperation from several people or groups to be successful

__ Innovation and synergy

__ Relatively quick assembly, deployment, and disbanding of people, as opposed to setting up more permanent structures and processes

__ Organization-wide representation, decision making, and buy-in

__ Mutual and shared, versus individual, accountability and ownership for the work done

__ If a team is needed, determine if there is already a group in place that can do this work.

__ Does the work call for the assembly of a special team?

__ Decide what type of team is needed:

__ Intact work team

__ Cross-functional team

__ Project, task force, or problem-solving team

__ Ongoing special team

__ Briefly describe the type of team that is needed. (For example, "We need a project-focused team with representatives from customer service, finance, personnel, and sales.")

__ Determine the best reporting structure for this team.

__ Who will lead or sponsor the team, what department (if any) will spearhead it?

__ To whom will the team report its results? (Remember to consider whether the reporting structure could hinder or sway the work of the team in a negative manner.)

__ Decide what degree of autonomy the team will have. (If you want an innovative, motivated, and empowered team, give it as much autonomy as the organization can afford. In many cases, this is where organizations need to compromise.)

__ Identify where budget support will come from.

Team Justification Worksheet

Use this worksheet to help you request the need for a team in your organization.

1. Briefly describe the work that needs to be done.

2. Explain why a team is the most effective way to get this work done.

3. Does the work call for the assembly of a special team or does a team already exist that can do the work?

4. What type of team is needed?

   __ Intact work team

   __ Cross-functional team

   __ Project team, task force

   __ Problem-solving team

   __ Ongoing team with special responsibilities in addition to regular work

   __ Other

5. What sponsorship or reporting structure will this team have? Will someone oversee the work of the team? If so, who?

6. What degree of autonomy is needed for this team to function well? What types of decisions will it be able to make and implement on its own? Which decisions must be approved?

7. Estimate the scope and length of the work (time frame, number of people needed, money needed, and so on).

8. Where will budget support for the team's work come from?

9. What other organizational goals will this work support? How should this team's work link to other work being done in the organization?

10. What results are expected from the team?

How to Select Team Members

Once the need for a team has been established, the next step is to choose the team members. First, it must be determined who will be responsible for selecting team members. If the team already exists as an intact work group, then membership is not an issue. However, when starting a new team, someone must be responsible for selecting team members. Generally, the person who established the need for a team will be involved in selecting team members, but not always. A team leader may be appointed and become involved in selecting members. Members may be asked to volunteer or even interview for team membership. In many cases, a person's position in relation to the work of the team will determine if he or she will be a member of the team.

Once the team charter is complete (see chapter titled *Step One: Focus the Team*), the team's membership may need to be reviewed by its current members. The team leader and team members can then decide if the current membership is adequate for the work of the team. Team members can suggest others to be invited to join the team or may suggest that certain members be removed from the team. Those working on selecting team members should keep in mind the expectations and reasons for the existence of the team. They will need to determine if the team members should come from the immediate organization or department, if the team should include internal or external customers or suppliers, if employees from other departments (e.g., finance or personnel) should be included, or if others who might have important perspectives or ideas should be included.

What Does the Work Require?

When forming a team, those selecting the team members should take into account what the team will need *as a whole* to function well. Some of these needs may be as follows:

- Technical knowledge and experience
- Coordinating and administrative abilities
- Team leadership skill and experience
- Team facilitation skills and experience
- Interpersonal and communication skills
- Prior team experience
- Knowledge of organizational goals and culture
- Variety of abilities and approaches needed to round out the team

Some typical team needs are as follows:

- People who will see the "big picture"
- People who will do detail work
- People who will coordinate and oversee progress
- People willing to be creative, as well as those willing to do the painstaking work of research and/or implementation
- Good representation of technical, relationship, collaboration, and communication skills
- People who will keep the team linked to the larger organization's goals and operations
- People who value consensus and are willing to work hard to reach consensus and come up with creative solutions

Advisors, sponsors, subject matter experts, or other support may need to be made available to the team on an as-needed basis.

What Size Team Is Needed?

One of the challenges teams face is the fact that the optimum size of an interactive, highly involved team is generally five to nine members. Teams with more than nine or ten members usually run into trouble when trying to coordinate and involve the entire team in problem solving and decision making. Sometimes task forces can be larger if much of the work can be done in sub-teams; however, the larger the team the harder it will be to coordinate the work. The temptation is for the larger team to meet infrequently, and this slows down the momentum of the team's work. Many work teams are already formed around the work itself, and the size of these teams may be fixed due to the way the operation is set up. In any case, organizations should try to keep the size of a team to five to nine members if the team will be innovating, solving problems, or making decisions. Implementation teams may need to be larger but must be coordinated.

Another membership concern to address is the location of team members. In many organizations, the most appropriate team may include people from different geographic locations. Some teams may even need to include members from throughout the United States or even from various countries. For example, one team in a large company included people from all over the United States who met quarterly as a task force to address diversity concerns and make and implement recommendations. This organization had world-wide responsibilities and was spread out across the United States. It had some diversity issues that needed to be addressed, and representation was needed from smaller field offices and from corporate headquarters. The team had to figure out ways to keep in touch by phone, e-mail, and internal mail.

Other teams may have to work from various facilities in one major metropolitan area. Still others may simply have to walk down the hall or to an adjacent building. More and more project teams include team members working from home. For example, recently a San Diego–based publishing firm was purchased by a San Francisco-based firm. During the involved relocation of the acquired group to San Francisco, editors, marketing personnel, and production employees continued working for months on projects with team members based in both cities. Though the methods of communicating differ when team members are separated geographically, the principles of effective teamwork remain the same. When forming a team, these concerns must be taken into account.

What Representation Is Needed?

Those selecting team members must consider several things:

- What type of representation (what functions, groups, knowledge, and skills) is needed?
- Who is needed on the team to make it successful?
- How can we have adequate representation without forming too large a team?
- If a large team (12 or more people) is necessary, how can we ensure small-team creativity, cooperation, and cohesiveness?
- How can we minimize the difficulties the team may encounter due to geographic separation? (For example, do we have an adequate budget for travel expenses so the team can meet as frequently as needed? Can the team come together for one or two significant sessions and achieve the major portion of its work?)

Another way to select team members (if a new team is being assembled) is to ask departments or groups to decide who they want to represent them on the team. In this case, the person assembling the team will work with managers and supervisors to select the most appropriate people. Again, it is important to get a *balanced* representation. Balance should be achieved in the following areas:

- Number of people from various disciplines or departments, for getting buy-in, viewpoints, doing research, and so on
- Technical knowledge and expertise (in relation to the work that needs to be done)
- Non-technical skills and experience, such as skills in leading and being on a team, communicating, facilitating, coordinating, project management, planning, presenting, writing, and working with computers
- Diversity representation (What variety of knowledge, skills, backgrounds, and other reference points might be beneficial to the team? It is a good idea to include someone new to the organization or someone with a different perspective for fresh insights.)
- Innovation skills and creative, big-picture skills
- Implementation skills, such as planning, coordinating, performing detail work, following up, and communicating
- Knowledge of the organization

Selecting Team Members

Once team representation is determined, it is time to begin to consider individuals who will fill the needs of the team. The following questions help determine if a particular person would make a good member for this team:

- How much does the person know about what the team will be working on?
- Does the potential team member have sufficient background and practical experience in the area the team will focus on?
- What technical skills and other resources can this person offer to the work of this team?
- Is the candidate free to work on the team? Does he or she have sufficient time to attend team meetings and do team tasks?

- What level of team experience does the person have?

- Has this person been successful interacting in a team setting before? If not, does he or she have a collaborative style of working—an ability to communicate effectively, listen, ponder, and come to consensus?

- Will this person's position in the organization help or hinder the team?

- Does the person have a genuine interest in the work the team will be doing and in being on the team?

It is unreasonable to expect that every team member will have a balance of the skills and technical expertise needed for the team. Instead, those selecting team members should aim for a balanced representation on the team. It may be necessary to include people with special knowledge or technical abilities who have had little experience working on a collaborative team. It is important in this case to ensure the team has other members who will support collaborative efforts and will facilitate the team's working together productively.

Following are three worksheets that may help select the members for a team: the Checklist for Forming the Team, the Skills List, and the Team Selection Matrix. These tools will help select a team with a good mix of skills, knowledge, and perspectives to ensure the team's success. If the team already exists, the team can use the matrix to determine its strengths and to identify any gaps that may cause the team difficulty. If there are serious gaps, the team can collaborate on ways to compensate. Some of the ways teams compensate are to add another team member, to invite a subject matter expert as a guest to some team meetings, and to agree to share among several team members the tasks that don't get done. The team should acknowledge its weak spots and be creative in trying to strengthen them.

Checklist for Forming the Team

__ Determine how team members will be selected:

    __ By invitation or appointment

    __ On a volunteer basis

    __ Through interviews with potential team members

__ Determine who will be responsible for team selection.

__ Decide what functional and technical representation is needed on the team.

__ Consider whether customers or suppliers (both internal and external) need to be represented on the team.

__ Determine what skills, knowledge, and experience are needed on the team.

__ Decide which advisors or sponsors should be assigned to the team as resources to be consulted on an as-needed basis. (Depending on the nature of the work, it may be better if the team decides this after it has written its charter. In some cases, team members can determine if advisors will be necessary.)

__ Determine what size of team is optimum for the work to be done.

__ Address any initial concerns about the geographic separation of team members, if applicable.

__ Consider what other diversity of team members might be desirable (e.g., various levels in the organization, ethnic and gender representation, someone new to the organization).

Skills List

Use the list of skills below to help determine what skills are most needed on the team. This is not an exhaustive list of team skills. You may need to add your own. Don't aim for perfection here. Use the list to get an idea of what's most important for the team.

L = low level of need
M = medium level of need
H = high level of need

	Level of Need (Circle One)		
A. Technical Skills (specify what type):			
_____	L	M	H
_____	L	M	H
_____	L	M	H
_____	L	M	H
_____	L	M	H
B. Project Management Skills:			
Planning	L	M	H
Use of computer planning software	L	M	H
Coordination	L	M	H
Pilot testing	L	M	H
Implementation	L	M	H
C. Collaboration Skills:			
Facilitation	L	M	H
Consensus decision-making	L	M	H
Conflict resolution	L	M	H
Listening and understanding others' views	L	M	H

D. Communication Skills:

Contributing and listening in meetings	L	M	H
Summarizing and checking for understanding	L	M	H
Sense of when to communicate information and to whom	L	M	H
Electronic mail	L	M	H
Presentation skills	L	M	H

E. Creativity Skills

Sees the big picture	L	M	H
Thinks outside boxes/paradigms	L	M	H
Innovates, comes up with realizable solutions	L	M	H
Patience with the creative process	L	M	H

F. Detail Skills:

Does accurate research and data gathering	L	M	H
Carries out detailed team tasks	L	M	H
Thorough, patient	L	M	H

G. Team Leadership Skills:

Initiates discussion and plans	L	M	H
Makes suggestions	L	M	H
Draws out other team members	L	M	H
Helps team move along in the process of its work	L	M	H

Team Selection Matrix

The purpose of this matrix is to help you get a balanced team. On the left side of the matrix the skills from the Skills List worksheet are listed. In the blank spaces, write in the skills that you believe are most important for the work of this team. Across the top, write in the names of potential team members. Write an X in the box when you believe the potential team member has strengths in that skill area. If you are interviewing team members, ask people where they think their skills are and then ask them to explain how they used that skill successfully in the past.

If your team already exists, you can use the Skills List and the Team Selection Matrix to see where you are strong as a team for the work you are doing and where there are gaps that need to be filled.

Skill	Name	Name	Name	Name	Name	Name

Overview of the Ten Steps

The most important goal of teamwork is to achieve results. Several things must come together before this can happen: The team needs clear goals, team members must collaborate and reach consensus, resources and support must be available, and plenty of coordination and communication needs to take place. This book will help your team pull all this together in a step-by-step approach.

Each step represents an important milestone in teamwork. When one milestone is overlooked or left uncompleted, the team will run into problems down the road. Following these steps will set your team up to move forward with a sense of direction and accomplishment. There are ten steps, or major milestones, to complete; these ten steps represent three phases of teamwork: getting organized, producing, and wrapping up.

Phase I: Getting Organized

Step One: Focus the Team

Step Two: Assign Roles

Step Three: Establish Ground Rules

Phase II: Producing

Step Four: Plan the Work

Step Five: Do the Work

Step Six: Review Team Performance

Step Seven: Complete the Work

Phase III: Wrapping Up

Step Eight: Publish the Results

Step Nine: Reward the Team

Step Ten: Move On

In general, each step must be completed before the team can move on to the next. However, in one instance, the team does not need to follow the steps in the order presented in the book. Your team may need to review its performance before reaching Step Six. Step Six is critical, however, because at some point the team will need to take time to review its work and effectiveness. Steps Four through Seven may need to be repeated several times before the team is ready to go on to Step Eight (Publish the Results). Some steps have sub-steps that must be taken before moving on to the next major step.

Every team is on a journey. A team needs a good map (orderly processes for working), travel gear (reliable resources), and reliable companions (healthy team relationships). When teams lack productivity or lose momentum, the problem usually stems from one or more of the following three things: (1) the team is not clear about what it should be doing; (2) the team lacks resources, knowledge, and tools for getting its work done; or (3) poor team relationships and members' behaviors are blocking team progress. Following the ten steps to teamwork will keep your team from falling into one or more of these "pits" and never getting out.

FIGURE 1 10 Steps to Team Results

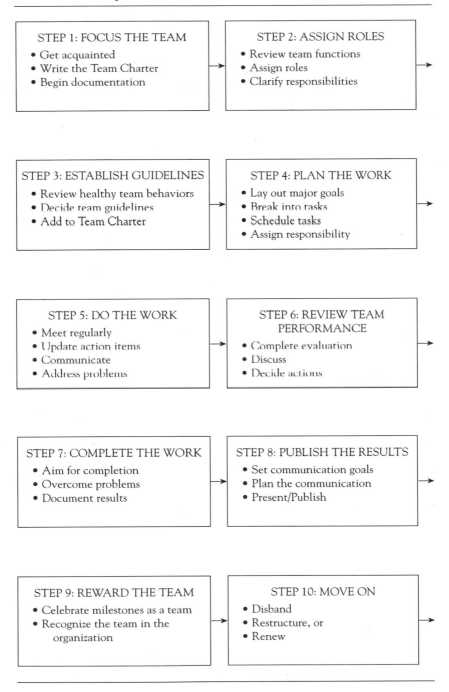

STEP 1: FOCUS THE TEAM
- Get acquainted
- Write the Team Charter
- Begin documentation

STEP 2: ASSIGN ROLES
- Review team functions
- Assign roles
- Clarify responsibilities

STEP 3: ESTABLISH GUIDELINES
- Review healthy team behaviors
- Decide team guidelines
- Add to Team Charter

STEP 4: PLAN THE WORK
- Lay out major goals
- Break into tasks
- Schedule tasks
- Assign responsibility

STEP 5: DO THE WORK
- Meet regularly
- Update action items
- Communicate
- Address problems

STEP 6: REVIEW TEAM PERFORMANCE
- Complete evaluation
- Discuss
- Decide actions

STEP 7: COMPLETE THE WORK
- Aim for completion
- Overcome problems
- Document results

STEP 8: PUBLISH THE RESULTS
- Set communication goals
- Plan the communication
- Present/Publish

STEP 9: REWARD THE TEAM
- Celebrate milestones as a team
- Recognize the team in the organization

STEP 10: MOVE ON
- Disband
- Restructure, or
- Renew

Phase I: Getting Organized

The first three steps in teamwork will get your team organized. During this phase, team members get acquainted, determine team goals, and establish ground rules for working together. In Step One, Focus the Team, team members get to know one another and lay out the team goals. In Step Two, Assign Roles, members are assigned team roles to help the team function as a unit. In Step Three, Establish Ground Rules, team members decide what they will hold one another accountable for and how they want to behave toward and support one another.

During this phase of the team's life, the team members will be seeking common ground and exploring the best avenues for succeeding as a team. Very little "real" work will get done during this stage of organizing and focusing. However, it is during this stage of teamwork that critical groundwork gets laid for achieving results as a team. Every team has to become comfortable with new relationships and ways of behaving before it can get much work done.

Step One:
Focus the Team

Teams become good at teamwork by doing things as a team. The first step in teamwork is to define the team's purpose and goals. During this step, the team members will answer these questions:

- What is our reason for being together as a team?
- What is our mission or goal?
- What do we want the results of our efforts to be?
- When do we expect to accomplish our mission or goal?

The answers to these questions will be incorporated into an important document, the team charter. Writing this charter is the most important thing to accomplish in Step One. However, several things must happen before the team is ready to write its charter. Depending on the experience level of your team, you will need to do some or all of the following:

- Make sure everyone on the team knows why the team was formed and what is expected of it.
- Review the definition and purpose of a team.
- Give team members a chance to get acquainted.

Once team members have been introduced to one another and know why the team was formed, work on the team charter can begin.

Announce the Reason for Forming the Team

Once the team members have been selected and before the team starts to work, a leader from the organization should meet with the team and explain why the team was formed and briefly outline what is expected of the team. The organization leader should specify how the team's work will affect the organization and the importance of the team's work. Provide some background information (perhaps a brief history of the situation) and describe the current environment in relation to the work the team faces. The team will need to know what, if anything, has already been attempted in relation to its project or work and what the results were. The team members will need to know why the decision to form a team was made and what is going on currently both inside and outside the organization that will affect the team's work. The leader's presentation should be brief, be as honest and straightforward as possible, and have a positive tone, so the team members will not be discouraged before they begin.

The organization leader should outline what plans are in place to support the team. For example, the leader could mention the kind of support that will be available; names of people who the team members can go to for help; and budget, facilities, and supplies that will be provided for the team.

Address the Issue of Empowerment

During the initial steps of teamwork, the question and topic of empowerment frequently come up. First, empowerment has become a much maligned, misrepresented, and misunderstood word. Many organizations have promised empowerment, but not delivered. Employees have asked for empowerment and then hesitated to take on the risks involved. Some employees began to resent management for making any decisions, because the employees were "empowered" to do so. Some people think empowerment is just another hollow term for the latest management and training fad. Others have seen attempts to empower teams and individuals fail because clear boundaries were not set up in the beginning, authority was not given, or people were not trained. In some cases, everyone had a different idea of what empowerment meant.

For the purposes of this book, I want to clarify what many organizations are successfully doing under the term empowerment. *Empowerment* means to give power or authority, to enable or permit. Many organizations see the need to drive power downward into the organization so that decisions can be made where there is appropriate information and projects can be implemented with the buy-in and involvement of those who must make them work. One of the most common ways organizations can do this is to create teams that have a defined amount of power and authority to decide, plan, and make things happen. After decades of living with a style of leadership that carefully guarded power and left decisions with management, transitioning to this new way of sharing power is difficult for many managers and organizations. However, many companies and managers today realize that in order to survive in the marketplace, people in organizations must be empowered to make decisions, to plan, and to act, without having to channel everything up through management.

Before an organization simply "empowers" a team, the leaders of the organization need to answer the following questions:

- What decisions will be the *sole responsibility* of the team?
- What decisions will be made *collaboratively* between the team and management?
- What decisions will be *reserved for management*, but *with* team input?
- What decisions will be *reserved for management*, but *without* team input?

It may be difficult for the leaders to answer all of these questions up front, but they should be asked, and asked again and again, until the team is clear to what extent it is empowered.

Empowerment does not mean the team will make all the decisions. An empowered team decides and directs those things that make sense for it to control, given the team members' level of knowledge and experience and given the direction in which the organization is moving. Teams that perform well will likely be given broader authority over time as they prove they can handle team decision making in a way that benefits the organization.

Empowerment is *not* abandonment. In some cases, management has "empowered" teams and then left them to flounder without direction, training, or support. Empowerment does not mean that management stays uninvolved or sets up teams to fail. Concerned managers will coach, sponsor, champion, and support the teams they empower. A function of management is to continually help teams define boundaries of power and to increase these boundaries when appropriate. Another function is to provide training so that teams and team leaders will succeed.

Empowerment *does* mean more individual responsibility for an organization's success. Employees who are used to letting management make all the hard decisions may lack the confidence to dive into a new realm of decision making.

The team may need to work with management and influence managers in deciding how much authority to give to the team. If the team leader is not clear about the boundaries of the team's empowerment, he or she should work with management to clarify areas that are "out of bounds" (i.e., areas that are not within the team's power to decide or control). The team leader should help management understand empowerment from his or her point of view and the leader should try to understand it from management's point of view. It is crucial to the organization that management and the team have a common understanding of what the team has the authority to do.

Review the Definition and Purpose of a Team

If some or all of the team members are new to working in teams, the team leader should briefly review the definition of a team and stress that the purpose of teamwork is *to work in mutual dependence to achieve results*. People have various degrees of success in teams, so by explaining what a team is and what is expected of a team, the leader gives members a sense of clarity and purpose.

It is important to stress that a team is a *group of people working together in a coordinated effort to achieve common goals*. If the people could accomplish the goals working separately, a team would not be necessary. An effective team produces results and becomes a cohesive unit through the process. The definition of an effective team can be expressed using the letters T-E-A-M as follows:

Two or more people working closely together

Encouraging and supporting one another to

Achieve—in an efficient way—

Mutually agreed upon and appropriate goals

To be "appropriate" the "mutually agreed upon goals" must support the goals of the organization and make a positive impact on overall organizational performance.

Katzenbach and Smith in their book, *The Wisdom of Teams*, emphasize that teams must not only have a common purpose, but must also be committed to common performance goals. They point out that the real purpose for creating a team is to achieve a result that will benefit the organization. "Performance is the crux of the matter for teams. . . . Real teams are much more likely to flourish if leaders aim their sights on performance results that balance the needs of customers, employees, and shareholders. Clarity of purpose and goals have tremendous power in our ever more change-driven world."[1]

[1]From Jon R. Katzenbach and Douglas K. Smith, *The Wisdom of Teams: Creating the High-Performance Organization* (Boston: Harvard Business School Press, 1993), pp. 12 and 13.

Team leaders must be careful not to predetermine a solution for the teams. Leaders can expect team results that will benefit the company, its customers, and its shareholders, *but leaders should not select a desired solution*.

> "Sometimes managers, thinking they already know what improvements need to be made in the process, pick a solution to be studied rather than a process. Instead of telling a team to come up with ideas about what change to make, they tell them what the results should be."[2] When leaders predetermine team decisions, solutions are often less than optimum, resulting in a misuse of company resources and low team morale.

Focus on Becoming a Total Quality Team

As the team leader and members set goals for the team, they should consider what it means to be a total quality team. In keeping with organizational efforts today to produce high-quality goods and services, your team, too, can benefit by focusing on quality. A *total quality team* is a group of people working interdependently to achieve increasingly higher standards of performance through continuous improvement in both cohesiveness and output. Such a team will produce predetermined results as a team, add value to the organization, be an enjoyable unit to work in, and continually improve its performance as a team.

Give Team Members a Chance to Get Acquainted

The team leader should let team members get acquainted in a way that puts everyone on common ground and makes people comfortable. To get off to a good start, the team must acknowledge every-

---

[2]Peter R. Scholtes, *The Team Handbook* (Madison, Wis.: Joiner Associates, 1988). Used by permission.

one's presence and begin to demonstrate that *every* member of the team has a valuable contribution to make.

In his book *Group Power,* William Daniels explains the importance of getting a group to the point where each member has equal influence. Otherwise, some members of the group will "spend a lot of energy trying to get a position of advantage from which to influence the group."[3] Group members may appear to "get right down to business, but, in fact,. . .will be working on a 'hidden agenda'—a contest to determine a 'pecking order' for the group." When this is allowed to happen, the natural resolution is for some team members to capture power and gain more influence than others.

A better condition for the team is for all members to have equal influence. At the first few team meetings, the team leader or the facilitator will need to conduct get-acquainted sessions and discussions in a way that gets *everyone* to speak up. This establishes that each person has value to the team.

An excellent way to balance influence on a team is to use a method William Daniels refers to as an "inclusion activity"—an activity that has "everyone act pretty much like everyone else for the first few minutes. Everyone sits in the same kind of chair, with an equal view of everyone else. Everyone takes a brief turn talking, for an equal period of time."[4] This is particularly important at the first meeting, usually during a get-acquainted activity. The leader of the meeting simply says something like, "Let's get acquainted by having each person tell us his or her name, work function, and location, and by saying a few words about how he or she came to be on the team." If the team members already know one another, this time can be spent with each person saying a few words about the team's assignment. For example, the leader of the meeting can say, "Since we all know each other, let's begin by each person saying a few words about your expectations for this team, and asking any ques-

[3]W. R. Daniels, *Group Power: A Manager's Guide to Using Meetings* (San Francisco: Pfeiffer, 1986). Copyright ©1986 by Pfeiffer, an imprint of Jossey-Bass Publishers.
[4]Daniels, *Group Power.*

tions you have so far. Just take one or two minutes." The leader then records the names, expectations, and questions, and briefly addresses them after everyone has spoken. Using this method includes everyone and gives the facilitator or team leader a chance to respond to each person's comments, which reinforces the importance of each member on the team.

During the life of the team, when the balance of power gets skewed, the team leader will need to facilitate an inclusion activity from time to time to bring everyone back into a position of influence.

Not only will the team leader have to handle people who want to capture all the power, the leader will also have to handle people who do not want to influence the team and who hold back and just want to follow along. Occasionally, a team member will refuse to contribute or contribute only when asked. He or she may either want the group to draw him or her in, or the member may be taking a wait-and-see attitude—thus, putting extra burden on the other team members. Members who hold back will hurt the team's progress in the long run, so the team leader needs to draw them in early and frequently. It is important that the members understand that contribution and active involvement are critical to the team's success.

Some team members may come from cultures that frown upon interrupting or speaking out in a group setting. Others may be naturally shy and hesitant to speak up. Having inclusion activities early on gives these people permission and encouragement to speak up during an open discussion, instead of holding back as they normally would. For example, one quiet team member did not get a chance to talk until an inclusion activity and then made a very valuable contribution. Once the team is accustomed to everyone speaking up, team members will begin to draw one another out because they are used to hearing from everyone.

A helpful way to introduce team members to one another is by using team member profiles. The team uses a form similar to the one that follows. Each team member is given a form and after the first few meetings, he or she completes a profile on every team member. By doing this, each team member gets to know other team members and learns the members' knowledge and expertise. The completed form also serves as a memory jogger.

TEAM MEMBER PROFILE

Name: Phone: Fax:
                                E-Mail:
                                Mailing Address:
 	
Current Function:
Work Experience:
Special Knowledge for This Team:
Misc. Notes:

During this early stage of teamwork, team members can expect to feel uncertain and tentative about their relationships with one another. Team members may have anxiety about their own knowledge, status, or role on the team. They may be concerned about the affect team responsibilities will have on their jobs. If the team is a natural or intact work team, being on this team *is* the members' job. This may make some members anxious about their own job performance, because it will depend on working well with others and on how well the team functions as a unit. As the work of the team progresses, team members will become more skilled at working in a team environment.

Resistance to Teamwork

No matter how hard your team tries, or how successful it is, some team members may still resist being on the team. Some people just do not trust teamwork and prefer to work alone. This is not surprising given that we are a nation of individuals, raised and trained to think, act, and learn on our own. Don't be surprised if one or more of your teammates either overtly or covertly resists being on the team. Sometimes resistance is very subtle and can be ignored while the team member adjusts and decides that being on the team is not so bad after all. Sometimes the resistance is open, annoying, and hurtful to the team.

Whatever the resistance, it will have to be dealt with as each situation happens. Usually, peer and management pressure are enough to influence people to give teamwork a chance. What draws them into the team is getting involved. This is another reason why it is important to get balanced participation as soon as possible.

Write the Team Charter

What Is a Team Charter?

The team charter is a document that declares the *mission* or *purpose* of the team, its performance goals, and what the *end product* of the team's work will be. The team charter may also include a brief *background* of the situation faced by the team, what *results* the team expects to achieve, a *projected date* for completing the mission, and constraints or *boundaries* the team must work within. Many organizations refer to this type of document as the team charter. Calling it a team charter focuses the team on the end results it expects to achieve. It can be thought of as a job description for the team and the team's performance agreement. Your team may call this document whatever makes sense in your organization, but the purpose of the team charter is to define what the team expects to achieve.

Some organizations require teams to complete a specific agreement or charter form, which may include other information, such as the names of the team members, sponsor, and leader; or a statement as to how the team's charter supports key organizational goals. Most teams want to include their ground rules in the team charter, once they are written (Step Three: Establish Ground Rules).

Purpose of Writing a Team Charter

Writing the team charter is perhaps the most critical activity the team faces, other than completing its work as a team. Writing a charter forces the group to agree on a common purpose, and the group's purpose creates the inspiration for the team's work.

To write the charter, the team must determine what its performance goals are.

> No team arises without a performance challenge that is meaningful to those involved. Good personal chemistry or the desire to "become a team," for example, can foster teamwork values, but teamwork is not the same thing as a team. Rather, a common set of demanding performance goals that a group considers important to achieve will lead, most of the time, to both performance and a team. Performance, however, is the primary objective *while a team remains the means, not the end.*[5]

The main purpose, therefore, of writing the charter is to declare what the team's performance goals are and what the team will do to justify being a team. The best teams tend to be those that seek to balance the needs of customers, employees, and shareholders. The second reason for writing a team charter is to focus the team. In today's world of more and more change, clarity of purpose and performance goals are essential. With a focus on clear goals and purpose, the team has an infinitely better chance of pulling together, working through differences and challenges, and achieving results, than a team without a clear purpose and goals.

Team leaders and team members may wonder why the person or group who authorizes the formation of a team does not just *tell* the team what its purpose and goals are. The process of developing a goal can be seen as counterproductive and a waste of time. After all, what if the team comes up with the "wrong" purpose and goals?

[5]From Jon R. Katzenbach and Douglas K. Smith, *The Wisdom of Teams: Creating the High-Performance Organization* (Boston: Harvard Business School Press, 1993), p. 12.

There are several reasons why a team needs to write its own charter. First, a team is frequently formed and authorized from a higher level in the organization that does not fully understand the scope of the work the team is being asked to do. Management may know there is a problem but not be sure what the problem is, or management may not really know what they can expect from a team project. The team charter is an avenue for the team to clarify what it can do and to help management define a realistic goal. Management's approval of the team's charter can be obtained before the team moves forward with its work. This does not mean that the team should discard the goal or purpose presented to it by management; instead, the team should work carefully to clarify and buy into the goal, put it in writing, and make sure the team and management agree to the goal.

The most common mistake made during this phase of teamwork is for the team to develop a purpose that, upon closer examination, was unclear, too broad in scope, or was redundant to a project already being done in the organization. For some teams, however, clear objectives do come from outside the team—from management, customers, or another team. When this happens, team members still need to discuss the objectives to understand them and to commit to them and to write a clear statement of purpose. Second, when team members write their own charter, they take greater responsibility for the team's success. Because team members will be doing the work, it is important that they be involved in defining the team's purpose. Only then will each team member know what the team's goals are and be committed to these goals. Having a commitment to common goals is one of the most important elements of an effective team. People may join a team to fulfill personal goals or hidden agendas. For example, a team member may join a team to gain stature or a promotion in the organization and may strive to take a leadership role on the team. This becomes a hidden agenda if the team member does not mention it to other team members but acts in ways to make it happen. Another team member may have joined the team thinking his or her pet peeve will get addressed. Someone else may have a solution to the team's work and expect to take a strong role in influencing the team in that direction. When team members struggle through the writing of the team charter, they are apt to set aside personal or hidden agendas and buy into the common goals of the team. This does not mean that a team member will not get personal needs met; it means that if his or her personal needs get met, it will be because doing so supports (or does not hinder) the mutually agreed-upon goals of the team.

The team leader can help the team understand the direction, boundaries, and expectations of the organization, but team members, selected because of their expertise and knowledge of the work to be done, must have a say in the team's purpose.

Third, when the team writes its own charter, members understand the team's purpose.

Whether or not the team's organization requires the team to submit a charter for approval, the team will need to develop its own charter. Some advantages of having a clear, written charter are as follows:

- A charter focuses the team members.
- Personal agendas are more easily set aside when a team has a clear charter.
- The act of writing the charter clears up misconceptions and confusion about what the team's purpose really is.
- The charter helps the team focus on what is important and keeps it from wandering off on tangents or aiming at too broad a purpose.
- The charter tells others in the organization what the team is doing. It spells out what the team's end product will be.
- The charter keeps others in the organization from giving extra work to the team. The team leader can explain that the team's mission does not include that work, even though that work may be valuable.

- The charter tells the team when its work is finished and whether it has succeeded.

- If the charter becomes obsolete, a new charter can be written. It is better to regroup and write a new charter than to start off without one.

The team charter is the foundation on which rests all of the team's work. The charter may get revised during the life of the team, but it is the cornerstone of the team's focus. Without it, a team is like a rudderless boat, drifting from goal to goal, from idea to idea, and from one problem to another.

Team Charter Definitions

Following are brief descriptions of items your team may want to include in its charter.

Team Name:	The name of the team, if the team chooses to have one.
Date of Charter:	The date the team charter was completed.
Team Members:	A list of team members' names. The team may also choose to have everyone sign the original copy of the charter.
Mission:	A brief statement that explains the purpose of the team. It can answer the question, What will this team do that no one else in the organization is doing? Most missions start with the phrase, "Our mission is to . . ."
Organization Fit:	What organizational goals does the team's mission support?

Performance Goals:	This defines, as clearly and measurably as possible, what results the team will achieve. It answers the questions, What will happen as a result of your team accomplishing its mission? What will improve? What will be different?
End Product:	Describes the team's *deliverable*. Spells out what your team's end product will be: a decision, a report, a recommendation, a completed event, a production level, a percent improvement, a successful implementation of a new process, and so on.
Background:	An explanation of the situation the team is facing. What is the recent history in relation to the team's assignment?
Ground Rules:	(These will be written in Step Three.) The rules of conduct for which team members will hold themselves accountable. General guidelines for how the team will work together. Describes which behaviors are appropriate and which are not.

To determine what information your team needs in its charter, the team leader and team members should ask the following questions:

- How much information do we need in the charter to give us focus and clarity?
- Who else will see the charter? How much information do they need to have?
- What do other teams in our organization include in their charters? Why?

When to Write the Team Charter

Once team members are acquainted with one another, and all members informed of the expectations of the team, the team should begin to write the team charter. Some teams assign team roles before working on the charter, but the team should wait until after the charter is written. This allows team members to become acquainted and to work together on equal footing for a time, regardless of current organizational positions or former levels of authority. It also allows the natural preferences and talents of members to come forth, which makes it helpful when assigning roles (Step Two). A facilitator is necessary to lead the charter-forming meetings, preferably someone outside the team, so all team members can be involved in deciding what the charter should be.

If the team leader has already been selected before the team begins to meet, the team leader should invite a facilitator to lead the initial team meetings. This allows the team leader to be a team member (with equal influence), while the facilitator guides the group to consensus. (More will be said about the team leader's and facilitator's roles in Step Two.)

How to Write the Team Charter

Team members usually groan when the facilitator says, "Now we are going to write our team's charter. We'll first start with determining what our mission is." They have reason to groan, because writing a clear mission and charter is hard work, and they may have past memories of endless meetings in which mission statements and charters were debated, hammered out, and nitpicked to death, leaving everyone exhausted and deflated.

To stimulate creativity and clarity when writing the team's charter, the facilitator should ask members to consider the following questions:

- What is our team purpose?
- What makes our team unique?

- What end results do we want to achieve?

- What are our performance goals? How can we state those goals so that others can easily measure our success?

- How is what we do essential to the organization?

- What end product(s) will we deliver?

- What is *within* the boundaries of our work as a team? What is *outside* the boundaries of our work as a team?

- Who are our customers (internal and external), and how will we serve them?

It is possible to come up with the team's charter relatively quickly, and a time limit should be put on this activity. Remember, the charter can be revised as needed. What the team needs as it begins its work is a good idea of what the team's work is. Writing the charter should not be crammed into a one-hour meeting, nor should it take marathon sessions to complete it. Following are some tips on how to write a good charter and minimize the time it takes to complete it:

- Set aside a meeting or two dedicated just to writing the charter. Emphasize the importance of everyone's attendance and involvement in this process.

- Ask a skilled facilitator to lead the meeting. The facilitator should be able to draw out everyone, record ideas, summarize, help the group consolidate its ideas, and bring the group to consensus.

- Do not get bogged down in "wordsmithing" (trying to find the perfect word or phrase). Instead, be content to rough out the wording at first and allow time for plenty of discussion as to what the wording means. The object is *general agreement* and *clarity*, not a literary document written for posterity. The right words will come later when the charter is reviewed and polished.

- After a rough draft is done, end the meeting. Review and polish up the charter at the next meeting. Try to refine the wording, but again don't waste time wordsmithing.

- If the team is large enough (more than seven people), divide portions of the charter (mission statement, performance goals, boundaries, background) among two or three sub-teams. Have each sub-team draft ideas for its portions of the charter. Then bring the whole team together, review the ideas, and make additions or changes together.

- Take the rough draft of the charter to a few appropriate people outside the team and get their feedback. Ask them the following questions: Is the charter clear? Will people outside the team understand it? Does it sound reasonable to you? What suggestions do you have? Bring these suggestions to the meeting when the team reviews and revises the charter.

- Once the team charter is written, make sure every team member has a copy. Give a copy of the charter to those people who need to be aware of the team's efforts (e.g., team sponsor, managers, customers, end users of your team's product). Circulating the charter will accomplish two facets of good teamwork: (1) regular documentation of the team's progress and (2) linking with those outside the team who will be important to the success of your team.

Once the team charter is complete, and signed off on (if this is necessary), the team has completed Step One. There are two things the team should begin doing during Step One: (1) begin documenting the team's work and (2) understand team decision making. This will help the team be efficient and productive and will begin to build cohesiveness in the team.

The Mission Statement

A good mission statement will keep the team focused and energized. Indeed, the mission statement is at the heart of teamwork: it will give life and power to your team's work. The team will need a mission statement in its meetings to stay focused, and the team will use it to communicate its purpose with others. The mission statement must be well-written, inspirational, motivating, realizable (not too broad), challenging (not too narrow or unimportant), and specific enough to differentiate the team's purpose from that of other teams and/or individuals in the organization.

A good mission statement should be brief, clear, and inspiring, and it should cover everything the team is doing. Keep the mission statement easy to memorize so team members can recite it when necessary. In addition, make it challenging enough to energize the team, but not so grand or broad that it is impossible to achieve. Too often, teams create long, flowery mission statements that are either vague and hard to remember or too grandiose to achieve.

It is tempting for teams to jump into action and bypass the arduous work of carving out their mission. But without a unity of purpose, the plans and actions of teams lack focus and lose momentum. Striving to write a clear, powerful mission statement forces teams to look closely at what is really desired, before planning how to proceed.

Following are a few examples of mission statements:

To work in partnership with the citizens of our city to improve public safety and the quality of life in our community. (A team of patrol sergeants of a police department.)

To promote the cultivation and use of diverse talents in our organization, to support a balanced life and successful career for every employee. (Diversity team within the division of a large corporation.)

To continuously improve yields, quality, and reliability in the production of our company's products. (Manufacturing operations team.)

To enhance the quality of life by providing proprietary health care products and financial opportunity through innovative research and uncompromising service.[6] (Manufacturer of health care products.)

To successfully launch the new order-entry system without decreasing our current output. (Project team.)

To introduce the new ZOZ product to the marketplace and raise sales to $1.5 million by the end of the second year on the market. (Sales and marketing project team.)

To provide high-quality, timely training to employees, which will enhance their ability to perform well on their jobs. (Human resource development team.)

Once your team has completed a draft of its mission statement, the team should continue working through the other portions of the team charter. The team can return to the mission statement and refine it, if necessary, once it has defined, or at least made a rough draft of, the other elements.

Checklist for a Good Team Charter

Once the team has drafted its charter, the facilitator or the team leader should check it to see if it meets the standards of a good team charter. A good team charter has the following qualities:

- Is clear and simple
- Is achievable
- Is bought into by the whole team
- Supports organizational goals
- Clarifies the team's task or role
- Communicates the team's purpose to others
- Is motivating to the team

[6]Actual mission statement of Mannatech Inc., Grand Prairie, Texas.

Begin Documenting the Team's Work

The team will need to keep a written record of its work. The team should keep a master set of documentation that represents all the important data used or generated by the team. This includes a brief summary of every team meeting, which in turn includes all action items committed to by team members. The team charter should be documented and a copy given to every team member.

In addition to the master set of documentation, every team member should have a team notebook, which he or she organizes and brings to each meeting. If the members receive or generate too much data, their notebooks can be cleaned out and older papers filed until the team's work is done, or until the papers are no longer needed. A notebook forces each team member to take ownership for knowing what is going on in the team and holds the member's material to support his or her team assignments.

FIGURE 2 Team Member Notebook

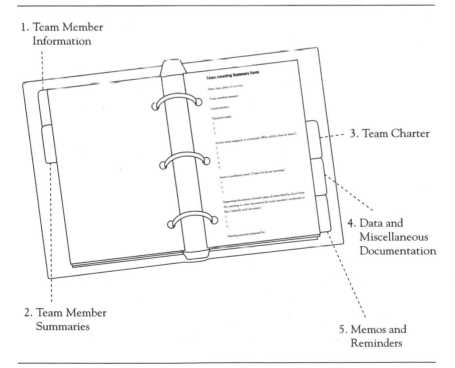

The advantages to having good team documentation are as follows:

- Reinforces what was done and decided at team meetings
- Reminds members of team decisions, action items, and commitments
- Saves the team valuable time from hunting for or re-creating data
- Keeps team members from wasting time on subjects already discussed. Team members can refer to earlier discussions on the same subject and save time rehashing it.
- Documents progress made on team goals.
- Informs organizational leaders of what the team is doing and what progress it is making.
- Provides material for team presentations, especially for when the team makes a final presentation of its results to management.

What to Document

The team should document the following information:

- The team-member names and telephone numbers where they can be reached (the team could include fax numbers and e-mail addresses).
- The team charter. (See the Team Charter Form at the end of this chapter.)
- A summary of every team meeting. (See the Team Meeting Summary Form at the end of this chapter.) After each team meeting, the team recorder can collect the flip charts and put the information on a word processor. (See the role description of the team recorder in Step Two.) The recorder's role is to transfer the exact wording of the flip charts, with minimal changes for clarity, and to complete the Team Meeting Summary Form. Copies are given to all team members. (If there

are a lot of flip charts, the team can decide at the end of the meeting what information to discard and what to keep.)

- Any important data *generated by the team*, such as results of research and analysis, recommendations, planning charts, and letters sent out. The team may decide not to distribute copies of this information to every member. For example, one team created a team box in which members stored a master set of all team documentation. The team box was brought to every team meeting. One backup copy was made of all documents used by the team, including data that was not copied for team members. If someone needed to use the data, only the backup copy could be removed from the box. All master copies had to stay with the box.

- Team presentations made to the team or by the team.

- Any important data *received by the team* to do its work. Again, not all such documents need to be copied for every team member. The team can decide who needs copies.

A team member should be appointed to be in charge of the documentation; it could be the team leader or the team recorder, or the job can be rotated. Whoever is responsible for the documentation must make sure that the master set of documentation is not borrowed. This is important, even though these documents could be generated should the team need them. Having a master set is more efficient than searching and waiting for data that may have been misplaced.

Once team members have gotten acquainted, the charter is written, and a documentation system in place, the team is ready for Step Two: Assign Roles.

Lessons in Teamwork

The team should take time during Step One to review Making Team Decisions and Holding Productive Team Meetings in the Practical Lessons in Teamwork section of this book.

Team Meeting Summary Form

Date, time, place of meeting:

Team members present:

Guests present:

Decisions made:
1.
2.
3.

Action items assigned, or continued: (Who will do what by when?)
1.
2.
3.
4.
5.

Issues or problems raised: (Topics for future meetings)
1.
2.
3.

Supporting documents: (Attach copies of transcribed flip charts from the meeting or other documents for team members' notebooks or files.) Identify each document.
1.
2.
3.

Meeting summary prepared by:

Team Charter Form

Team name: Date of charter:

Team members:

Mission statement: Our team's mission is to . . .

Performance goals: To achieve our mission, we have set
                         forth the following performance goals:
                         (The goals should be achievable and
                         measurable, with a targeted date for
                         completion.)

Organization fit: Our mission supports the following
                         organizational goals and/or values:

End product: The end product our team will deliver
                         is: (e.g., a decision, a recommenda-
                         tion, a completed event, a project
                         implemented, a percent improvement,
                         dollars saved)

Team guidelines: We will follow these ground rules
                         while working together as a team:

Background: (Briefly describe the recent history or
                         situation in relation to the team's
                         assignment.)

Signatures: If desired, have each team member
                         sign the original copy of the charter.

Step Two:
Assign Roles

The next step in teamwork is to determine who will function in what role. Your team will function better if team members are clear about what role each person is filling. Role assignments do not need to be permanent and they can be shifted from time to time. However, it is important that every team member know who is playing what role when.

The purpose of Step Two is to determine who will fill general team functions so the team members perform well as a team. More specific responsibilities, those related to the team's actual project or work, will be determined by team members later during the planning and doing phases of the team's work (Steps Four and Five). Sometimes, the team leader will have already been chosen by the team sponsor, or a facilitator may have been selected for the first meeting. Once either of these roles have been filled, the team leader can begin assigning roles to the team members. Over the life of a team these general, assigned roles may rotate, but at any given time, everyone on the team must be clear who is assigned what team role. For example, the role of facilitator may change for every meeting, and this change should be announced clearly at the beginning of each meeting.

The team should take a little time to consider the differences between traditional work, in which individuals report to a manager or supervisor, and teamwork, in which a small group of people (a team) is held responsible for defined segments of work. The following chart includes common beliefs on traditional work and team work. The team should review the chart and consider other ways in which the two approaches to work differ.

Traditional Work	*Teamwork*
Individual accountability	Mutual accountability
Individual goals	Shared team goals
Focus on individual performance	Focus on team performance
Independence	Interdependence
Infrequent, unfocused interaction with peers	Frequent, focused interaction with peers
Individual jobs defined	Output of team defined
Competition valued and encouraged	Collaboration and cooperation valued and encouraged
Functional roles given to groups and individuals	Teams take on several functions
Individual, professional skills needed	Teams skills also needed
Headset: Please your supervisor	Headset: Respect your teammates
"This is my job."	"This is our job."
"This is not my job."	"How can I make the whole team successful?"

Review Important Team Functions

The following functions are common and important to all teams:

- Coordinating the team.
- Keeping the team focused on its tasks.
- Keeping the team focused on working together as a team.
- Facilitating team meetings.
- Documenting of team efforts.

- Supporting the team in the larger organization.
- Collaborating and reaching consensus.
- Communicating with team members.
- Communicating with people outside the team.
- Contributing and participating in team efforts.
- Carrying out assignments and commitments.
- Seeking resources and support.

Review Common Team Roles

The following roles are common for most teams in organizational settings:

- Team leader
- Team facilitator
- Team member
- Team sponsor (or mentor, advisor, coach, champion)
- Team recorder

Some teams combine the role of recorder with that of the facilitator or leader. In the early stages of a team, the team leader and/or sponsor will usually decide who will fill what role. Later on, the team may decide to rotate roles.

It is important to distinguish the role of team leader from that of a traditional supervisor or manager. The team leader's key role is to be member of the team. The team leader takes a leadership role in coordinating and supporting the team, but *not* in making decisions. When the team makes decisions, the team leader participates as a team member. The team leader is also a spokesperson for the team, a resource seeker, and a link to the rest of the organization. It is generally easy for team members to comprehend the new role of team leader as opposed to supervisor or manager. But it is sometimes difficult for the *leader* to let go of the pattern of leading by directive or by stepping in to make decisions when the team struggles. The team leader's role can be a difficult one to fill. It requires balancing the role of coordinating with the role of team membership.

In organizations accustomed to teamwork and in experienced teams, members become skilled at the various team roles, and the role of team leader can be rotated among members. This works well, *if* each selected team member is clear about what the role of team leader is. In organizations new to teams, the team leader should be someone who is comfortable and skilled at allowing team participation in decision making, and who is capable of filling a coordination role as well. New team leaders need training and grounding in the role, particularly if adequate role models are not present in the organization. Once team-leader role models emerge, training new team leaders becomes simpler. Team members who have seen an effective team leader in action will find it easier to fill the role than those who learned without role models.

Overview of Each Team Role

Following is a brief description of each role as it has been used successfully in various organizations. A more complete description of each role is included at the end of this chapter.

Team Leader

The team leader's role includes four parts: (1) to manage and coordinate the team so that it gets its best work done, (2) to provide resources to the team, (3) to link the team and its work to the rest of the organization, and (4) to be a contributing team member. As coordinator of the team, the team leader's responsibilities include coordinating the team's meetings, making sure that administrative details are completed, and overseeing the team's activities. The team leader ensures that team records are kept and that all important documentation is available to the team as needed. As resource provider, the team leader makes sure that the team has adequate meeting facilities and supplies, as well as money for other necessities. The team leader is the main channel between the team and the rest of the organization, and in this capacity, the leader alerts the team to changes or problems in the system that affect the team. When possible, the team leader removes blocks and barriers to the team's success. "Ultimately, it is the leader's responsibility to create and maintain channels that enable team members to do their work."[1]

The role of team leader is a critical one. Without the role of team leader, important administrative and coordinating details may not get done. In most cases, each team member will assume someone else will do them. Someone needs to be the focal point for the team's communication and connection with the rest of the organization.

In more mature, high-performing teams, rotating leadership is practiced. Different members, depending on their knowledge or experience in leading a group, lead the team for a period of time. When training teams and team leaders, the organization or the facilitator should decide whether the team leader should facilitate the team's meetings. This will be discussed later in this chapter.

Team Facilitator

The team facilitator's main responsibility is to facilitate the team meetings, keeping team members focused and ensuring that all members are encouraged to participate. The facilitator remains neutral as to the content and decisions of the meeting, but takes an active role in managing the process of group discussion and decision making. The facilitator should be skilled at facilitating group discussions, providing structure and methods for the team to get its work done, and listening to and summarizing what has been said. In

[1]Peter R. Scholtes, *The Team Handbook* (Madison, Wis.: Joiner Associates, 1988). Used by permission.

addition, the facilitator organizes and summarizes inputs from the participants in such a way that the team can use the inputs to set goals, make plans, make decisions, and solve problems.

Team Member

Team members are selected for a team because they have a particular skill, expertise, or experience to contribute. Therefore, a key role of the team member is to contribute fully in his or her specialized area. In this way, the team member will help the team get its tasks done. Just as important as making a contribution in a specialized area, however, is to contribute to the overall productivity of the team. A good team member strives to be an objective listener and to help the team reach consensus. Team members carry out assignments, meet commitments to the team, ask questions, listen to teammates, work diligently toward consensus, gather data, attend team meetings, communicate with team members, and carry out numerous other functions to help the team keep its momentum and achieve results.

From time to time, team members fill the role of team leader. Also, members with facilitation skills and experience are good candidates for facilitating team meetings, although no one team member should facilitate most of the team meetings. In the neutral, facilitator role, the team member cannot contribute opinions and ideas on the subject. (See the discussion on the team leader as facilitator of team meetings later in this chapter.)

Team Sponsor

Also called the team mentor, team champion, team coach or team advisor, this person's role needs to be defined by each organization, and sometimes by each particular team. Some teams do not have a team sponsor. Generally speaking, the team sponsor provides overall organization, direction, and support to the team and is not an active member of the team. Unfortunately, the sponsor often becomes too distant from the team, even to the point where some team members do not know who their sponsor is. The sponsor may be the person who justified the need for the team, selected the team leader, and paved the way politically and financially for the team to get started. The sponsor acts as advisor to the team leader, when needed, and supports the team by being available as a resource. The sponsor should attend some team meetings to show support and learn about the team's progress. In some organizations, it is crucial to have a sponsor who will intervene for the team. The sponsor is frequently a higher level manager with a stake in the team's performance and results.

Team Recorder

The team recorder captures the team's ideas and key discussion points on a flip chart, or white board, for all to see. The record serves the team in two ways: (1) he or she provides the team with a working document (some people call this the *group memory*) to use as it proceeds through its work, and (2) he or she maintains the records of what was done and decided at the meeting. The recorder role is crucial because inputs must be recorded accurately, fairly, and without bias.

The team recorder and facilitator are often one and the same, because most facilitators are trained to record as they facilitate. It is not always productive, especially for a small team, to have one of the team members act as recorder, because while recording the team member needs to remain neutral and is busy capturing the points being made. This leaves a team member out of the discussion and decision making. Many teams regularly rotate this role, and it can even be rotated during a team meeting, if the meeting is long enough. In any case, the team leader or the team members should not appoint a member as recorder if he or she has important contributions to make on the topic at hand . The facilitator is probably the best recorder because he or she is forced to listen well and summarize. When using someone else to record, the facilitator must frequently coach the recorder and watch to see that important thoughts are captured. During lengthy or difficult discussions, the facilitator may ask someone else to record so the facilitator can observe team-member behavior more closely and keep better eye contact with the group.

Some teams appoint a timekeeper who helps the team set time constraints and keep track of time during team meetings. When the team gets bogged down or runs behind, the timekeeper alerts the team and the facilitator. A skilled facilitator can also function as the timekeeper, but some facilitators and teams prefer to have someone else watch the time.

Address Typical Role Problems in Teams

Who Will Facilitate Team Meetings?

One of the most difficult decisions for new teams to make is who will facilitate the team's meetings? Should it be an outside facilitator (should it be someone who is not a team member but an employee of the organization, or a consultant)? Should the team leader facilitate team meetings? Should team members rotate the role of meeting facilitator?

Teams do better when they have a neutral facilitator at most of their meetings, especially during the start-up period. Outside facilitators also work better for team meetings. For example, one organization put considerable effort into selecting and training a reservoir of team facilitators who facilitated team meetings throughout the organization. A designated percent of their time on the job was devoted to facilitating team meetings outside their own immediate department (to help them maintain neutrality). The organization made a conscious effort to place team facilitators with teams removed from the facilitator's areas of expertise, which made it easier for the facilitator to focus just on the process of the team meetings.

When to Use a Facilitator

If possible, the team should use a facilitator (someone other than the team leader) when the team is getting organized and dealing with the many issues of start-up: assigning roles, writing a charter, developing team ground rules, establishing meeting times, getting acquainted with one another, setting initial goals, and planning. Once your team is settled in and functioning, the team leader or a team member can facilitate the meetings. However, the team will sometimes need a skilled, neutral facilitator at its meetings—someone not caught up in the issues the team faces. Your team should use a facilitator during the following situations:

- When there are a lot of opinions or data on an issue
- When team members disagree or are stuck in conflict
- When the team has difficulty achieving a balance of participation
- When every team member's contribution and focus is needed on the issue at hand
- When special group methods are needed, and team members are not skilled in these methods
- When the team has lost momentum or clarity and needs some outside guidance to get it back on track

Most team leaders are chosen for their knowledge of the team's area of focus, not for their skill as a facilitator. It is difficult for anyone to facilitate (i.e., remain neutral) when a team is discussing items of interest and concern to the facilitator. In addition, team leaders with subject-matter knowledge are needed by the team to contribute as an active team member. However, if the team leader was chosen because of his or her facilitation skills, and not because of his or her subject matter expertise, then the leader could function as the meeting facilitator. While facilitating, this team leader may occasionally want to add an opinion or idea. If the facilitator does this, he or she should give the team an advance explanation and should be brief. The facilitator-leader should say something like, "I'd like to step out of my facilitator role for a minute and express an opinion." Once finished, the facilitator-leader should clearly step back into the role of facilitator and alert the team in some way, perhaps by saying, "I'm stepping back into my facilitator role now."

When to Use a Recorder

As a rule of thumb, only use a recorder when it makes the team more efficient and productive. When the team does use a recorder, the team leader should make sure the recorder can capture ideas briefly and accurately, can remain neutral, and does not take over the facilitator's role. Ideally, the facilitator and the recorder will work smoothly together, and the recorder's efforts will free up time and energy for the facilitator to carry out his or her role more effectively.

Should the Team Leader Be the Team Expert?

Another role concern that frequently comes up in teamwork is if the person who is an expert in the team's subject matter should be or can be a good team leader. If the team leader is the key expert, will his or her workload be too heavy, and maybe impossible? What will serve the team best? These questions should be addressed early on so the team gets off to a good start.

Team members should keep in mind that the team leader's main role is to coordinate the team's efforts and to keep communication and other channels open for the team to do its work.

Finding and Using a Facilitator

Where to Find a Facilitator. One of the common problems teams face is where to find a facilitator with adequate skills and time to help the team. Most teams cannot assume that there will be a trained facilitator available within the organization, with time to dedicate to the team. There are three places your team can look for a facilitator:

- Within the team
- Outside the team and within your organization
- Outside your organization

Using Someone on Your Team to Facilitate. The facilitator may be the team leader or a team member. This is probably the most common, and expedient, solution to the problem of finding a facilitator. There are a few drawbacks to this approach, although it is certainly preferable to not having a facilitator. In fact, teams without some kind of facilitation will face serious roadblocks to team success. If the team uses its team leader or a team member as the team facilitator, it should keep in mind the following:

- The facilitator's main role is to facilitate the team meetings, and in this capacity should remain neutral.
- Be sure the team facilitator understands the importance of remaining neutral and using effective facilitation methods during the team meeting (such as recording team inputs for all to see, explaining and facilitating the use of group methods, keeping the team focused, and asking the group for consensus).
- Do not select someone to facilitate who is essential to the content of the team discussion or decision. For example, do not select the key expert on the current topic to be the facilitator.
- If possible, rotate the role of facilitator when the team is using the team leader or a team member to facilitate. This way, no one on the team has to remain neutral all the time.

- Budget and plan to train one or more of your team members and team leader in facilitation skills. Use them as role models for the rest of team members to learn how to facilitate.

- Make it a team expectation that several or all of the members will learn facilitation skills.

A good resource for teams who must look within the team or the organization for facilitation is Dennis C. Kinlaw's book, *Team-Managed Facilitation*. Based on the assumption that teams "are capable of managing every aspect of their own development and performance," Kinlaw offers teams a model for facilitating their meetings in which designated facilitators (from within the team), as well as team members, take ownership for successful meeting results. In this way, both designated facilitators and team members facilitate the meeting by following a model for successful team meetings. Everyone on the team becomes a resource and takes part in creating the conditions for a successful meeting. Designated facilitators and team members contribute to a meeting's success by doing the following:

- Use the model to keep focused.
- Clarify desired meeting outcomes, norms, roles, agenda, sequences, and processes.
- Identify resources needed.
- Practice quality communication.
- Build understanding.
- Provide structure.
- Use rational processes. Keep inputs relevant.
- Use interventions to move the team along.
- Identify issues that need to be addressed.
- Evaluate the performance of the meetings.
- Plan meeting improvements.

Kinlaw points out that there are really three outcomes to a successful team meeting. "Typically we think of success in terms of performing the tasks that the team sets out to perform. . . . The three results that should characterize successful team meetings are:

- Performance of tasks;
- Further development as a team; and
- Improvement of team meetings."[2]

Successful teams will aim to accomplish all three outcomes, and successful team members will practice behaviors, methods, and processes that will facilitate (make easier) the progress and achievements of their team. Kinlaw's book is a good resource to increase the team's competence level in managing its own facilitation.

Team members who work with skilled facilitators (whether from inside or outside the team) naturally develop facilitation skills over time. Team members who have been exposed to quality facilitation may begin facilitating from the sideline, suggesting approaches, refining processes being used, asking for others' inputs, or seeking consensus. When a facilitator is absent, a team member may temporarily take over the facilitation of a team meeting, or a portion of a meeting, using the skills he or she has seen the facilitator use. Some teams need minimal intervention from the facilitator, because everyone on the team is facilitating in some fashion or other. Indeed, the role of the team member, in this chapter, has several ways in which the member facilitates the performance of the team.

There are a few drawbacks to using someone on the team to facilitate, but they can be overcome. First, whoever is facilitating must remain neutral and, thus, cannot contribute substantially to the content of the subject at hand. This leaves the team with one

---

[2]Dennis C. Kinlaw, *Team-Managed Facilitation: Critical Skills for Developing Self-Sufficient Teams* (San Francisco: Pfeiffer, an imprint of Jossey-Bass Publishers, 1993). Used by permission.

member, or the leader, not participating in the decision or issue being discussed. The facilitator must either agree to support whatever the team decides or take time to give his or her inputs and buy in to the decision. The team needs to consider whether it is worthwhile to give up the input of one of the members in order to have a facilitator from within the team. The best way to overcome this is to train several people on the team to facilitate and rotate this responsibility.

Second, sometimes team members are not skilled enough to facilitate a particularly complex meeting or issue, when advanced facilitation skills are required. The best way to overcome this is for the team or team leader to determine before the meeting whether advanced facilitating skills are required for a particular meeting.

Third, for important, sensitive, or particularly decisive issues, team members will find it difficult to act as neutral facilitators. The team member–facilitator may inadvertently, or purposefully, try to sway the outcome of the meeting. In such cases, the team should have someone from outside the team facilitate.

Finding a Facilitator within Your Organization. Depending on the team's organization, finding a facilitator within the organization could be more difficult than using someone on the team to facilitate. Unless the organization has some employees who are trained as facilitators who will be available to teams, your team will have to find these people.

First, the team leader should ask the team sponsor, managers, or human resource professionals if the organization has facilitator resources. In large organizations, human resource professionals, trainers, managers and supervisors, team leaders, internal organization development consultants, and quality assurance professionals are frequently trained and skilled in facilitation. If your team is fortunate enough to have skilled facilitators in its organization, the team leader should find out the following:

- How to obtain them
- In what capacity they can help the team

- How much lead time they need to schedule time for the team
- How much of their time the team can expect to have and for how long
- Where to turn if the team has a crisis and needs a facilitator immediately
- If there is a charge for internal facilitator services

When working with an internal facilitator, who is not a member of the team, the team leader and the members should keep in mind the reality of the situation. If that person has another "real job," the team should determine how much of the person's time it can use. If the person has many responsibilities, the person may not be able to spend a lot of time with the team. However, if the person's key role in the organization is to facilitate and help teams, the team leader and the members should meet with that person and collaborate on how they can best meet one another's needs. Both parties will be in the fortunate position of being able to help one another succeed.

Using a Facilitator Outside Your Organization. If there are few or no facilitator resources available in your organization, your team may need to seek an outside facilitator, at least for the start-up of the team. First, the leader should check to see if there are funds available, because outside facilitators will charge fees for their services. If management does not want to spend money for a facilitator, following are some ways your team can negotiate permission and/or funds to bring in outside help:

- Show management how hiring an outside facilitator will, in the long run, save your team valuable time and money.
- Explain why the team needs a facilitator (e.g., no one on the team is trained or experienced, the team cannot spare anyone on the team to facilitate, a skilled facilitator will help get the team on the right track and keep it focused, other teams that didn't have facilitators really struggled).

- Show specifically how the cost of hiring an outside facilitator will be realized in savings to the company (e.g., higher quality, a key problem solved, an important decision made, the team's work being completed in timely fashion).

- Ask why management does not want the team to use an outside facilitator. Then see if you can overcome these objections.

- Ask management for permission to try a facilitator for the first phase of the team's work. Report your team's progress to management and point out how the facilitator helped. Management can decide whether to allow the team to continue using outside help.

- Bring evidence from other teams that have used an outside facilitator that this type of help is worth the cost.

- Ask an outside facilitator to give a brief presentation to your team and management on how outside facilitation can benefit the team.

- Simply include facilitation costs in the team's initial budget proposal and avoid the long discussions over whether to use outside help or not.

How to Select an Outside Facilitator. If the team is permitted to look outside for a facilitator, then the challenge will be where to find such a person. The team should begin by asking other teams, groups, or managers in the organization for recommendations. The team should also ask people in professional associations for recommendations. Go to human resources and ask for names of consultants who have facilitation skills. The team should make it clear what type of person it is looking for. Share with others the team facilitator role description in this book, or make up one. The team should not assume people will know what a facilitator is. There are many types of outside consulting services available to organizations, and the team needs to be clear about what it is looking for.

Before your team begins looking for an outside facilitator, it should decide who will be responsible for coordinating this search and who will make the final decision. Will the whole team be involved? How? Will the team leader make this decision? Will anyone outside the team be involved? Will someone outside the team need to make the decision or approve the decision?

Once a decision has been made as to who will coordinate the search and make the decision, the designated member can begin looking. The following two paragraphs will help the team member choose the outside facilitator.

When the member contacts a potential outside facilitator, he or she should have a list of questions ready to ask the facilitator. The member should tell the candidate the team is looking for someone to facilitate the team, and ask the candidate what experience he or she has had in this area. Avoid telling the candidates up front exactly what the team is seeking, in case the member meets someone who claims he or she can do whatever the member puts forth. If, without hearing the team's specifications, the candidate mentions having done many of the things the team is looking for, then the candidate probably has a clear idea of what team facilitation is about. The member should then ask the candidate what team facilitating he or she has done, how he or she went about it, and what the results were. (There are a few in every profession who tend to inflate their abilities, and it pays to use wisdom and caution when evaluating someone's level of experience.) The member should list as many of your team's expectations as possible before calling candidates. The member will also want to know about the candidates' availability, schedule, fees, special skills and approaches, and so on.

Following are some things the member should look for when hiring an outside facilitator:

- Find someone you can understand and who clearly answers your questions. If someone confuses you, tries to impress you with jargon and terminology, be cautious. You may have trouble working with them. Your initial conversation will often indicate what type of working relationship you will have.

- Find someone who listens well and asks questions about the team and organization.

- Find out what other teams or groups the person has facilitated and ask for references. Call and find out about the facilitator's approach, methods, and style. Consider whether this approach will fit the team and the organization.

- If you think you might hire this person, find out when he or she is available and whether he or she could meet the team's schedule. Sometimes outside consultants are too busy to adequately meet the team's needs, and you will want to know this before spending too much time evaluating their experience.

How to Work with a Facilitator

The team should not expect the facilitator to do meeting follow-up, recording of meeting notes, and other administrative duties. Someone on the team, such as the team leader and team recorder, should take care of these coordinating functions. For consistency, the team should try to have the same facilitator at each of its meetings, unless some special issue or occasion calls for a change. This will give consistency and flow to your team's meetings, and you will save time educating different facilitators about the team. If the team is following the ten steps outlined in this book, the team leader should give the facilitator a copy of the book and inform him or her where the team is in the process. The facilitator also will need to have copies of past meeting notes, the team charter, and other important documents or pieces of information. If the team is just starting up, this is the ideal time to bring on a facilitator, acquaint him or her with the process in this book, and begin working with him or her at Step One.

Experienced facilitators are usually knowledgeable about planning a productive meeting. If the team's facilitator is knowledgeable in these areas, the team leader and the team members should also be involved in deciding and planning team meetings. This develops team members' skills in planning meetings and increases buy-in to the meeting agenda. If the facilitator is not skilled at designing meetings, the team will need to plan its own meetings, evaluate the meeting (as suggested in this book), and make adjustments until the team's meetings are productive and results-based. When team meetings are not productive, teams are generally unproductive as well.

Whatever the skill level of the facilitator and your team, it is important for the team to continually collaborate with the facilitator in deciding what approaches to take, how much time to allot for agenda items, and what the team wants to accomplish in the meeting. In reality, the facilitator is a key member of the team, whether or not they are team member.

Assign Team Roles

When deciding who should fill what role, the team or the team leader should go over the functions of each role and ask, "Given the functions required of this role and the subject matter the team will be dealing with, who is best suited to fill this role?" If someone on the team is a subject matter expert or is highly skilled in the area the team will focus on, it makes sense to let them be a fully contributing team member—not the team facilitator, and maybe not even the team leader.

Once roles have been determined, the team should discuss each role briefly, including what the role is, why it is important, and what the team expects of each role. Questions or concerns about the various role should be addressed as they arise.

Clarify Responsibilities of Each Role

The role descriptions that follow are meant to be guidelines for your team. If they do not fit the team's needs, change them. If the team decides to change them, write them down and give every team member a copy of the revised role description.

Lessons in Teamwork

Sometime during Step Two, the team should review the lesson Capitalize on Team Diversity included in the Practical Lessons in Teamwork section of this book.

Team Leader

Role: Manage and coordinate the team so that it gets its best work done, provide resources to the team, link the team and its work to the rest of the organization, and be an active team member.

Tasks: Some of the tasks the team leader performs are as follows:

- Report team progress to the sponsor, or others outside the team.
- Set up team meetings, notify team members, secure facility and supplies, and see that team meetings are effective.
- Keep the team focused on what it is supposed to be doing.
- Define the team's boundaries to the team (i.e., what the team is expected/not expected to do).
- Keep open channels of communication between the team and the organization.
- Act as a project manager for the work of the team.
- Procure resources for the team (e.g., facilitator, supplies, subject matter experts, funding).
- Clarify organization's expectations of the team.
- Explain and, if necessary, defend the process the team is using to get its work done.
- Ensure team productivity.
- Contribute to the work of the team (as a team member) without dominating or over-influencing.
- Make sure team members are clear about their individual action items and commitments.
- Make sure team efforts are documented and made available as needed to the team, team sponsor, and (when used) the team facilitator.
- When possible, remove blocks and barriers to the team's success.

Challenges: Some challenges the team leader may face are as follows:

- Getting full attendance at team meetings
- Defending the team's decisions to others in the organization
- Contributing without dominating
- Being clear about what is expected of the team
- Creating realistic meeting agendas
- Balancing team leadership with team membership

Team Facilitator

Role: Provide the team with processes and structure in which to get its best work done. Lead the team's meetings, when needed, so that the best decisions are reached. Manage the process of group discussion and help the team understand its own needs and dynamics. Guide the team in making the changes necessary to become a cohesive team. Be the recorder during group discussions or help the recorder carry out his or her role. (The facilitator must understand the importance of and use of the recorded data.) Help the leader and the team set and keep to realistic time frames for completion of team activities.

Tasks: Some of the tasks the team facilitator performs are as follows:

- Help the team leader plan the initial team meetings.
- Facilitate the team meetings.
- Model and teach productive meeting behaviors and processes.
- Guide the team until it becomes adept at planning its own meetings.
- Encourage open channels of communication among the team members and between the team and the organization.
- Facilitate the team in evaluating its own progress as a team.
- Suggest group processes that will help the team do its best work.

The facilitator usually plays the key role in leading the team's meetings. This involves many tasks, such as:

- See that the team uses the most effective methods to gets its work done, with time to consider ideas and alternatives.
- Select from a variety of group process tools and methods, depending on what the work and the team's experience call for.
- Remain neutral on the content of the team's meeting, while taking an active role in guiding the process.

- Draw out everyone and balance the participation as much as possible.

- Encourage dialogue among team members, not between the facilitator and the team members. (This usually means simply being quiet and allowing team members to respond to one another.)

- Ensure that different points of view have been aired and considered.

- Record, organize, and summarize the team's inputs; post these in front of the room so all can see.

- Manage meeting time wisely. (As the meeting progresses, let the team know where it stands on time. When the team is planning its next meeting, give the team feedback on how long certain agenda items have taken in the past. Give the team a warning when it is going over the allotted time on a particular item, or when it is nearing the designated ending time for the meeting.)

- Listen actively to all team members.

- If someone else is recording, make suggestions to the recorder when necessary.

Challenges: Some challenges the team facilitator may face are as follows:

- Minimizing his or her own participation in the discussion
- Staying neutral, especially if he or she is vested in the outcome of the discussion
- Selecting the best processes for the team's tasks
- Maintaining balanced participation.
- Setting a tone that encourages openness and acceptance
- Creating realistic meeting agendas
- Helping teams struggle through their conflicts and disagreements

Team Member

Role: Contribute knowledge, experience, time, and support to both the team's work and the building of a cohesive team, so that the mutually agreed upon goals of the team are achieved.

Tasks: Some of the tasks the team member performs are as follows:

- Attend team meetings.
- Contribute to team-meeting discussions and decisions in a productive, positive way.
- Carry out action items and assignments as promised to the team.
- Offer support to other team members.
- Ask questions and listen to teammates.
- Share relevant information with the team.
- Help the team leader, facilitator, and sponsor in their roles.
- Speak up with own opinions and feelings, make suggestions, and ask important questions of the team.
- Do not hold up team progress by repeating ideas over and over. Let them ride on their own merit.
- Use professional skills and experience (e.g., organizing abilities, computer knowledge, technical expertise, people skills) to help the team be productive.
- Contribute to the work of the team without dominating or over-influencing.
- Make an effort to hear and understand teammates' points of view.
- When possible, remove blocks and barriers to the team's success.

Challenges: Some challenges the team member may face are as follows:

- Attending all team meetings
- Keeping team confidentialities (not mentioning things in the organization that will hurt the team or members of the team)
- Contributing without dominating, or taking the risk to speak out—whichever is more difficult
- Working hard to come to a consensus decision, especially when it is not the decision the team member wanted
- Fully supporting team decisions

Team Sponsor

(Coach, Champion, Mentor, Advisor)

Role: Provide overall direction, support, and encouragement to the team and ensure that the team's efforts support organization goals. Act as an advisor to the team when needed, or intervene for the team in the organization. Coach and collaborate with the team leader to set clear boundaries for the team, as well as give the team necessary leeway and authority to get its work done. Be available to the team as a resource.

Tasks: Some of the tasks the team sponsor performs are as follows:

- Attend some team meetings; show support.
- Find resources for the team when needed.
- Coach, encourage, and support the team leader.
- Help the team leader define team boundaries.
- Open channels of communication between the team and the organization. Keep the team leader informed.
- Clarify the organization's expectations of the team.
- Explain and, if necessary, defend the process the team is using to get its work done.
- When possible, remove blocks and barriers to the team's success.

Challenges: Some challenges the team sponsor may face are as follows:

- Supporting the team without interfering
- Letting the team come up with its own solution
- Being clear about what is expected of the team
- Keeping up to date and informed of the team's progress

Team Recorder

Generally, this role works best when merged with the facilitator role, but for some teams it works best to have both a facilitator and a recorder.

Role: Record key points in the discussions and decisions of a team.

Tasks: Some of the tasks the team recorder might need to perform are as follows:

- Remain silent on the content of the discussion.
- Accurately record key words and phrases as closely to the speaker's words as possible (so as not to alter the intended meaning).
- Write legibly and large enough for all to see.
- If necessary, ask team member to summarize comments so they can be recorded.
- Get help with spelling, if needed.
- Organize the data so it can be used efficiently by the group (e.g., title the charts, show where each different idea begins, indent, number points, use bullets, arrows—whatever helps the group see the relationship of the material).
- Tear off and hang the charts so they can be referred to as needed. Get help posting them, if necessary.
- Be careful not to leave out someone's idea or point.
- Know when to sit down and let the group discuss without recording. It isn't possible or necessary to record every point.
- Organize the charts and see that they are documented and copied for every team member's use.

Challenges: Some challenges the team recorder may face are as follows:

- Remaining neutral
- Capturing ideas accurately
- Organizing and labeling material
- Handling the flip charts
- Handwriting and spelling
- Knowing what to record and what not to record

Natural Team Roles

As the team works together, team members naturally take on other constructive roles, which help the team accomplish its goals. These "natural team roles" emerge from individual team members' natural tendencies in a group. They come about because people have different group skills and needs, and because the team needs someone to fill many of these roles. Following are some of the common natural team roles, though this is certainly not an exclusive list:

Suggestion Maker—This person, concerned with getting the job done, will offer suggestions as to how to proceed so the problem will get solved.

Summarizer—This person attempts to summarize what has been covered or what has been going on in the team.

Information Seeker—This person asks for facts, opinions, feelings, and alternatives, to keep the team functioning.

Topic Guardian—This person tries to keep the group from going off on tangents.

Gate Keeper—This person brings others into the discussion.

Clarifier—This person attempts to help others clarify their ideas and makes sure everyone understands.

Harmonizer—This person smoothes over the team's rough spots and tries to maintain a friendly, harmonious atmosphere.

Humorist—This person relieves tension with a joke. This is not the same as someone who continually disrupts the team with wisecracks and inappropriate joking.

Includer—This person draws in team members who are quiet or who have been left out of the discussion, and makes sure no one is overlooked.

Gate Closer—This person cuts others off, interrupts them, or ignores comments they make.

Devil's Advocate—This person constantly presents objections or identifies holes in the team's thinking. This can be productive when used sparingly and with care, but halts team progress when overdone.

Step Three:
Establish Ground Rules

Once the team charter has been written and team roles assigned, the team then needs to establish general ground rules for how it will operate and behave as a team. These ground rules, or norms, as some teams call them, serve as standards for which team members will hold one another accountable. In his book *Work Teams That Work*, Anthony R. Montebello refers to these standards as "working agreements"; they define what is acceptable and what is not acceptable in the way of team behaviors or practices:

> At the micro level, working agreements define how the team will communicate, coordinate, and work together primarily during team meetings. . . . At the macro level, the team must have direction on issues like how performance will be appraised, how rewards will be allocated, and how the team will work with other units. . . If the team does not take the initiative to develop working agreements, norms will emerge sanctioning undesirable behavior (e.g., it's all right to be 10 minutes late for meetings).[1]

---

[1] Anthony R. Montebello, *Work Teams That Work* (Minneapolis: BestSellers Publishing, 1994). Used by permission.

Developing team ground rules sets the foundation for trust, one of the most important ingredients of team success. "If the group is to perform effectively, it must be allowed to develop a climate in which members trust each other enough to be willing to share information, and to honestly critique each other's ideas."

Review the Purpose of Ground Rules

The main purpose of ground rules is to clarify the standards team members want to uphold. The rules become the behavioral guidelines of the team. They actually serve as a kind of "verbal contract" that team members make with one another. The ground rules spell out expectations for how the team will work together and serve as a standard against which the team can measure itself. If necessary, the team can change its ground rules as it learns from experience as a team. All teams work with standards or norms. Proactive teams define them; others just let them evolve.

There are several advantages to taking time during an early team meeting to set up ground rules. First, it causes the team members to think about what kind of team they would like to work on and how that team might operate. Second, it clarifies what the team members expect of one another and creates ownership and buy-in to these standards. Third, it is a proactive way to influence the team's successful performance. When ground rules are not discussed or set up at the beginning of a team's development, standards will simply be the *result* of how the team operates, not the way it *planned* to operate. A team without ground rules runs the risk of letting bad habits develop, which are hard to change.

Team members need to establish ground rules as a team and not rely on a team leader to tell them how to perform and behave. When a team sets its own standards, and revises them as needed, it is more apt to adhere to those standards and to police itself along the way.

Hold a Ground Rules Discussion

Setting up ground rules does not have to be a difficult or lengthy process. A simple discussion and agreed-upon list are sufficient to begin with. With a proper introduction to what ground rules are by the facilitator or the team leader, along with some examples, a team can probably brainstorm and come up with its ground rules in a one-hour meeting. It could take less time or more, depending on the nature and experience level of the team. Some teams have successfully come up with ground rules and finished their charter (when the charter was drafted at a previous meeting) in the same meeting. Another team included its operating ground rules in its charter and did all of this in a two-hour meeting. Other teams may need to take a full day to finish the charter and address ground rules.

There are several areas that a team can cover when setting its ground rules or norms. Following is a suggested list:

- Team meetings

  How frequent?

  Should they be regular?

  What attendance standards will the team hold to?

  How will the team handle differences of opinion?

  What standards of behavior will the team hold to during meetings?

- Communication between meetings

  What method of communication will the team use?

  When is communication necessary?

  Who initiates communication among team members?

- Behaviors toward one another

  What behaviors are inappropriate?

  What behaviors will the team strive for?

- Workload issues

    How will the team distribute work?

    How will the team members support one another?

- Team problems

    What problems does the team anticipate and how will the members work through them?

    How will the team handle rumors, confidentialities, and conflicts?

    How will the team handle team membership, for example:

    Recruiting new members

    Members dropping out

    Unwilling team members

- Will the assigned team roles be rotated or fixed?

These are just suggestions to stimulate the team members to think about their guidelines. All of the issues listed do not have to be covered, nor should the team attempt to cover all of them if they already have some ideas. The value of establishing ground rules in a team setting is to steer the group toward operating and behavioral standards that are agreed on by all members.

Review Healthy Team Behaviors

When the team is deciding its ground rules, it is a good time to review constructive and destructive team behaviors. For example, the team members should consider what behaviors build up the team and make it more productive, and what behaviors lead to divisiveness and apathy?

Every team member is responsible for his or her own behaviors on the team. Each member should focus on minimizing behaviors that undermine the team and maximizing behaviors that build up the team. Team members' behaviors can be separated into three major types:

1. Behaviors that contribute to the *cohesiveness* of the team
2. Behaviors that contribute to the *productivity* of the team (behaviors that focus on the task at hand)
3. Behaviors that *undermine* or *block* team progress (behaviors that hurt team relationships or block the effective completion of the team's tasks)

Some behaviors that foster team *cohesiveness* are as follows:
- Showing acceptance and understanding of others
- Relieving tension
- Showing energy and enthusiasm for the team's work
- Including all team members in discussions or events
- Listening and responding to others
- Building on one another's ideas
- Being at ease with opposite views and opinions
- Showing interest in and understanding of others' views
- Asking other team members what they think
- Attending team meetings and events
- Volunteering to take on team assignments or help others with their team assignments

Some behaviors that contribute to team *productivity* are as follows:
- Analyzing the data and facts
- Suggesting alternatives
- Testing for consensus
- Building on others' ideas
- Clarifying ideas
- Suggesting processes that will help the team complete its tasks
- Asking others for their opinions and ideas
- Offering information and data

- Summarizing
- Keeping the discussion focused
- Proposing creative alternatives
- Asking questions to help the team move forward
- Showing patience in dealing with complex problems
- Applying own expertise to the problem at hand

Some behaviors that *undermine* or *block* team progress are as follows:

- Disagreeing without offering suggestions
- Refusing to listen to other team members
- Repeating own ideas or opinions over and over
- Criticizing others' ideas or processes
- Interrupting
- Refusing to let go of a dead-end discussion and move on
- Dominating the discussion or trying to over-influence the decision
- Withdrawing
- Not being open during the team meeting (reserving candid comments for hallway meetings or sub-team discussions apart from the team meeting)
- Not showing up for team meetings or events
- Showing tension or disapproval
- Not cooperating
- Refusing to go along with any of the alternatives
- Impatience with the team process
- Excessive clowning around or vying for attention
- Demonstrating an attitude that "nothing will work here"
- Giving in, faking support of the team, or just being there because you have to

The team could probably add many more items to all three of the lists. In fact, a good introductory exercise for setting ground rules that the facilitator could conduct is to label three sheets of flip-chart paper. One sheet should be labeled cohesiveness, one should be labeled productivity, and the third should be labeled undermine. Let team members write their responses on the charts. Then the facilitator should read over the charts and ask team members to comment on the answers and on the members' comments. The team then selects ground rules from the ideas generated.

Decide Ground Rules

The team is now ready to decide its ground rules. The facilitator should check to make sure everyone agrees on each guideline. Once a list of ground rules has been agreed on, the rules should be listed on a flip chart for everyone to see.

Caution: The team should not simply copy another team's ground rules. This defeats the purpose of the "verbal contract." Each team should discuss and come up with its own ground rules by consensus.

Add Ground Rules to the Team Charter

Once the ground rules have been determined, they can be added to the team charter and posted at the team's meetings to remind members of agreed-upon standards. From time to time, the team should review its ground rules. The team leader, or the facilitator, can ask the team:

- How well are we following the ground rules we established?
- Do we need to change how we are working together?
- Do we want to add, change, or delete any ground rules?

Sample Team Ground Rules

Following are some ground rules followed by teams:

- Have regularly scheduled meetings.
- Team members should arrange their schedules to attend all team meetings.
- Begin and end meetings on time.
- Hear one another out at meetings.
- Speak out; avoid harboring hidden agendas.
- When confused, ask.
- It's okay to disagree, but not okay to discount or put others down.
- Offer suggestions rather than criticizing.
- Be open to different views. Try to see the merit in another's opinion.
- Recognize individuals for the contributions they make.
- Communicate openly and frequently between meetings.
- Use e-mail when all members need the information.
- Anyone can initiate communication.
- Keep shared confidentialities *within* the team.
- Ask for help when you need it.
- All members share in the work of the team.
- When we reach a decision impasse, we will try to create a new solution, or we will delegate the decision making.

Once the team has established its ground rules, the team is finished with the first phase of teamwork: getting organized. The team is now ready to tackle the "real" work, which is the reason it came together in the first place. Some people may wonder why all this work at the beginning is needed. If the team is created to work, why doesn't it just get to work? It can be done that way, however, whenever a team just starts doing its work, the team soon reaches a serious block to getting work done. Sometimes the team has put in hours and hours of work to no avail, because it simply cannot proceed. This may be because the team's mission or purpose is not clear, in which case, team arguments begin over what should be done, what the team's goals really are, and what the team was assembled for in the first place. Problems may arise over roles. For example, a team leader may take an authoritative position, or may not understand the nature of teamwork. Team members may not understand the importance of their roles on the team. The team may be meeting without a facilitator. Informal norms may develop that are destructive to good teamwork. For example, members may begin discounting one another, vying for influence, or getting stuck on their own pet solutions.

Doing the necessary up-front work will not eliminate all of the team's problems or those listed previously, but it will lessen them. By doing the up-front work, the team will have a stated mission or purpose to refer back to when it gets confused. It will set standards by which team members agree to operate. It will help everyone carry out his or her team role. And it will give the team something to measure its success against. Even though the getting-organized phase takes time, it is time well spent. Team members are also getting used to working with one another during this time. They learn to be productive as a group, so that when it is time to do the work, they are already experienced at reaching consensus. More importantly, if the getting-organized phase has gone well, the team members are already functioning as an effective team and will have less difficulties achieving results.

Most teams have trouble when they bypass the important, initial work of organizing. Sometimes, a team that gets off to a poor start never recovers. Bad feelings develop, and no real work ever gets done.

Celebrate Completion of the Team Charter

Congratulations! At this point in time your team has completed a major piece of work: writing its team charter. This is an opportunity for the team to celebrate and acknowledge completion of the first major hurdle in teamwork. Team members should read "Celebrating Team Milestones" in the Practical Lessons in Teamwork section of this book and do something to reward themselves for their fine work so far.

Lessons in Teamwork

Now is also a good time for the team members to review the Understanding Group Dynamics lesson included in the Practical Lessons in Teamwork section of this book. Just as it helps parents and teachers to understand stages of development in the lives of children, it also helps team members and leaders to be aware of how groups function in organizations and how teams develop over time. A little understanding in the area of group dynamics and development will provide encouragement and awareness to the team that will keep it from giving up on itself.

This is also a good time for team members to read the Team Member Credo in the back of the book and discuss it briefly at a team meeting. A couple of good discussion questions for the team are as follows:

- What aspects of the Team Member Credo did we cover in our ground rules?
- What other qualities do we, as team members, need to be aware of as we proceed?

Phase II: Producing

During the second phase of teamwork, your team will do whatever work is necessary to realize its mission as a team. During this producing phase of teamwork, the team will plan, do, evaluate, and correct its work. More than likely, the team will cycle through these four activities—planning, doing, evaluating, and correcting its work—several times before its mission is accomplished.

What is planned or scheduled by the team must be acted on or done. What gets acted on or done must be reviewed, debriefed, and evaluated so your team can replan, make corrections, and continue getting its work done. Few teams experience a smooth implementation of their plans. Plans must be reviewed and revised in light of actions taken.

The team needs Steps Four, Five, Six, and Seven to keep up its momentum and to reach its goal. All four steps are critical and interrelated. The team may have to recycle through Steps Four, Five, and Six several times before reaching Step Seven when the work gets completed.

Step Four:
Plan the Work

Up to this point, your team has been organizing and putting processes in place to function as a team. The team is now ready to plan how it will proceed. The team should keep in mind its team mission and ground rules as it plans.

The planning process described here is a general one that applies to both a project team—one whose job is to begin and complete a project, solve a problem, make a decision, or plan an event—and an ongoing work team. As an ongoing work team, the team will probably have a more broadly defined mission than a project team, and the team's major steps may be goals it plans to achieve in an upcoming work period such as a quarter, a year, or longer. If the team is a project team, its mission may be more narrowly focused and its planning stage may be shorter.

Whatever type of team it is, the initial planning session is needed to get the team started. If your team is an ongoing work team, it will need to hold periodic planning sessions to keep it on track. Whether the team is a project team or an ongoing work team, it will continue to plan as it goes through its work as a team. Indeed, the team will undoubtedly be planning at every team meeting. This initial planning session will be a baseline plan, and from there the team will adjust its plan as necessary.

In general, there are four major steps to this stage of planning:

1. Lay out major steps or goals that will accomplish the mission.

2. Break down each major step or goal into manageable tasks.

3. Lay out a time line for completion of goals and tasks.

4. Assign each task to a team member.

In reality, one-time planning is usually not enough. Planning continues until the mission is completed. However, in the beginning, it helps to complete as much of the overall plan as possible. The team may need to draft a list of steps or goals and tackle the first one or two before clarifying all the other steps or goals. In some cases, it is impossible to see ahead enough to determine what steps must be taken.

Lay Out Major Steps or Goals

The team should hold a team meeting specifically to plan, or begin planning, how it will do the work. During this team meeting, the facilitator or the team leader should post the team's mission and ground rules for easy reference. The facilitator should ask, "What major goals or steps must we take to accomplish our mission?" Once the goals or steps have been identified, the team may need to prioritize them and possibly delete some of them. Because your team will want to be efficient, it will probably select only those steps that are essential to accomplishing its mission.

The team should lay out steps or goals that the team can accomplish in a relatively short period of time. Goals that require too much time to accomplish can diminish team enthusiasm and momentum. The team should break down long-term or larger goals into sub-goals, or interim targets, on which the team can focus. Once these sub-goals have been accomplished, the team can determine what other goals must be accomplished to fulfill the team charter.

If it is difficult to develop a short-term goal, establish a long-term one, then work backward. Ask, "What interim targets do we need to achieve in the next 4 to 6 weeks that will find us well on our way toward long-term success?"[1]

The team should remember that for a goal to be effective it has to be measurable. When your team writes out its goals, it should be sure to include in the goal statement a measurement method. This is the only way the team will know—beyond a shadow of a doubt—that it has reached its goal. It will also help the team to measure just how close it came to reaching its goal, if the team should fail to fully achieve it. The team may fall short by only a small percentage point or dollar amount. A clearly written, measurable goal will give the team a definite target to shoot for. Following are some examples of measurable goals:

- Develop the new product according to customer specifications and within budget by June 15.

- Sell five systems to at least two different companies by the end of this fiscal year.

- Run the pilot training course and make revisions to the program so that it is available to all target audiences by December 1.

- Decrease response time to customer requests by at least 50 percent by the end of Q1.

- Put a system in place to keep response time at this level or better by the end of Q2.

Break Major Steps or Goals into Tasks

Once the team has determined what its major goal is, the team should break down each major step or goal into manageable, discrete tasks that can be assigned to team members. As the team does this,

[1]Anthony R. Montebello, *Work Teams That Work* (Minneapolis: BestSellers Publishing, 1994). Used by permission.

it will realize that some steps need to be done before others can be begun or completed. Each task may require the completion of several sub-tasks. Depending on the number of major steps or goals the team has targeted, it may make sense to pick one or two to work on before determining tasks for the others.

Schedule the Tasks

Scheduling is the secret of making things happen. It is said that planning is only the intention to do the work, while scheduling is a commitment. Things that are scheduled are more likely to get done, and on time; things that are not scheduled may never happen.

Once action items are assigned to individuals, your team needs to set deadlines for each task. These dates will become the time line the team will follow as it does its work. This schedule will undoubtedly have to be altered as the team works. One activity that the team will have to conduct at each team meeting is to update the schedule.

Some tasks will be dependent on other tasks; in other words, one person may not be able to complete his or her task until another person's task is completed. When the team creates a schedule, it must take these dependencies into account and note them in some way on the schedule. Your team should create a master schedule that lists all planned tasks and their due dates and the person responsible for completion.

Without this schedule, the team will have a plan without power. The schedule becomes the tool that puts the team's plan into action.

Once the team's initial planning session is complete, it will begin Step Five, Do the Work, and from then on the team will be planning the work, doing the work, planning again, working some more, and planning again. Steps Four and Five are iterative processes. After the first planning session, the subsequent planning is usually not as extensive. However, from time to time, considerable replanning may need to be done. Some events that may trigger replanning are as follows:

- Major company or department reorganization
- External factors that make the team's mission obsolete, such as changes in customer demand, competition, technology, management demands, and so on
- Discoveries made by the team that make its mission, or previous plans, obsolete or unworkable
- Significant changes in authority, resources, or information that affect the team or its mission

There are valuable planning models and tools available to teams today. Depending on the nature of the team's work, it may want to use an existing model as a basis for its planning. There are models available for problem solving, decision making, and process improvement. If a team member knows of processes that have worked for other teams, or that work particularly well in the organization, the team should use those processes. For example, the organization may have provided special training for the team in problem solving. This would be a good time to use it.

Use Scheduling Tools If Needed

As the team plans, it may need to take advantage of proven scheduling tools like a Gant or a Pert chart. A *Gant chart* is really a matrix that shows the action items or activities down the left column in relation to a time line, which is laid out across the top. Each activity's start and finish time is represented by a shaded horizontal bar, or line. Some activities are dependent on others being completed before they begin, and the Gant chart accommodates this nicely. A *Pert chart* lays out the flow of the major activities in a kind of pictorial map, or several paths, using nodules for each activity. The map is laid out so that everyone can see what activities can be done in parallel and what activities are dependent on others. It also shows what activities come first and estimates the time needed for the various activities. The longest path (the one that takes the most time) represents how long it will take to complete all the activities, or the entire project. Another tool for planning is a Planning Time Line. To create a Planning Time Line, the facilitator or the team leader should draw a long line across the middle of several pieces of flip-chart paper and post them on the meeting-room wall. This list becomes your team's project's time line. The team members can show the flow of time by placing dates along the line. The team can draw lines up and down from the time line and label them to represent when important tasks must be completed. The team can also write in the name of the person responsible for each task's completion.

Posting your team's time line ensures that everyone sees it and agrees to it. The facilitator or team leader can place several flip charts side by side, and involve everyone in laying out the plan. Once the master plan is created, it can be transposed to a computer and copies made for everyone.

There are software programs that lay out Gant and Pert charts automatically as data is input. Changes can be made easily and copies reprinted for team members. By using a software program, the team leader or the recorder will not have to transcribe the plan. If the team meets in the same room for each meeting, and the room is not used by other people, the posted copy may be the only one the team will need. Few teams have this luxury, however, so most teams have to copy the plan so members can carry it with them.

Assign Each Task to a Team Member

The final step in planning is for the team leader to assign each task or activity to a particular team member. Many teams refer to these activities or tasks as *action items*. Once your team has laid out a general plan for its work, the leader should begin assigning tasks to individual team members. After the general planning has been done, the leader should ask the team: What are the first actions we need to take? Who will be responsible for those action items? What is the deadline of each action? In other words, *who* will do *what* by *when*. The leader or recorder should post the list of action items for everyone to see and record them in the team documentation.

Even if more than one person will be working on a task, only *one* team member's name should be placed beside the action item during planning. That person will be responsible for seeing that the task gets completed. Remember, "we" never gets anything done. If the team leader assigns a task to several people, one person may wait on another to see that the work gets done, confusion may result, things will not get done, and the incomplete activity may throw the whole team behind schedule. The team leader should emphasize that once a person accepts an action item, it is his or her responsibility to see to it that the work gets done or that team members are notified of any delays, if there are any. At each team meeting, while the team is doing the work (Step Five), the team will review its action items to determine whether they have been completed or not. The team will make necessary adjustments to its plan as it goes along. When action items are not completed on time, the team may need to arrange for increased support or effort, obtain more resources, assign more people to help, or replan. More will be said about following through on action items in the next chapter.

Ten Tips for Successful Team Planning

Planning does not have to be a long, drawn out process, but the team should give it adequate attention so that it builds a solid foundation on which to begin its work. Following are some tips to guide your team in its planning stage:

- Dedicate a meeting to planning how the team will achieve desired results.
- Use proven planning tools and models, especially those the team knows work in the organization.
- Begin planning at the macro level then move to the more detailed, or micro, level of planning. End the planning session by assigning specific action items to individuals.
- Keep the team's mission and ground rules in mind.

- Capitalize on the diversity and variety of strengths and talents among the team members, especially when assigning action items.

- Do not assume that people with technical or specific knowledge in an area should be the only ones with assigned tasks or responsibilities. Sometimes it helps to have an inexperienced view as well.

- Do not overlook assigning tasks to more than one person, but always make one person ultimately responsible for seeing that the work gets done.

- When assigning responsibilities and action items, try to avoid segmenting the team by the way you divide up the work. Try to keep team members interdependent. The more they work together the better they will operate as a team.

- Plan for more time than you think you need to complete the tasks.

Planning is a tool, not the end product. Make the plan work for your team, and adjust it as needed. It is not sacred, your results are.

There are several good planning resources available to teams. Some of these are included in the Readings/Resources list at the end of the book. There are methods to help the team set goals, make decisions, plan a project, plan a presentation, or improve a process.

Step Five: Do the Work

Once the team reaches Step Five, it should truly begin to be productive, provided it has successfully completed Steps One through Four. By this step in the team process, a successful team is both highly task oriented and highly person oriented. Group morale is high and group loyalty is strong. Differences in members' goals and styles do not get in the way of accomplishing team goals, and personal agendas are acknowledged and accepted but do not block team progress. Individual members feel secure in the group, individuality and team identity are both high, and creativity and collaboration are the norm.

By the time the team has reached this step in the process, most team members will be more than ready to begin doing the "real work" of the team. Depending on the nature of the team, members may be working geographically near one another on a daily basis, or they may be separated so that they will need to plan regular meetings just to see one another. Some teams are so scattered geographically, that they must do a considerable amount of planning to meet. In such cases, team members also incur travel expenses when they need to meet. Whatever the case may be, it is critical during this step in teamwork that team members communicate with one another and coordinate their tasks.

Teams that do not communicate and coordinate their work inevitably lose momentum, go off in the wrong direction, or simply waste valuable time because of miscommunication or misunder-standings. During Step Five, several things must happen. The team must review action items, plan them, and update the action items regularly in light of the original goals and plan. The planning done in the previous step may have to be altered, based on new informa-tion or events. Team members need to take ownership for the com-mitments they have made to the team and, in some cases, organize and present material they have found to the team. During this phase of teamwork, it is important that the team do the following:

- Hold regular, productive team meetings.
- Assign tasks to take advantage of team members' strengths and diversity. Share or rotate less desirable tasks.
- Make sure someone takes responsibility for overall coordina-tion of the team's efforts.
- Communicate frequently *between* meetings (both inside and outside the team).
- Review and update action items regularly.
- Replan when necessary.
- Document the team's progress.
- Deal openly with problems that stall the team.

Team members have important responsibilities during this phase of teamwork. Those teams whose members pull together, sup-port one another, meet individual commitments, and keep com-munication open during this time can become high-performing teams. Some important responsibilities team members have during Step Five are as follows:

- Take on action items appropriate to your strengths.
- Take on some action items that will force you to learn new skills.

- Volunteer to help other team members.
- Make every effort to meet your commitments, even if it means asking for help when you run into difficulties.
- Follow up with other team members. (Return their phone calls, provide information they need, inquire as to how their work is going, offer support and suggestions, and build on what other team members are doing to help your team be efficient.)
- Strive to provide quality, on-time work to your team.
- Speak up if you have a question, a suggestion, or a concern. Do not let the team's work slow down because no one spoke up.
- Maintain healthy working relationships with team members.
- Bring concerns before the whole team, rather than talking privately with some of the members.
- Share in the less desirable tasks your team faces. Do not expect one person to do all the unpleasant work.
- Try to communicate regularly with every team member, as opposed to leaving some people out and favoring others.

Remember to ask questions and listen. This is a wonderful way to build trust and rapport with your teammates. (They will be more apt to listen to you in the long run, as well.)

Meet Regularly

After the team has held several meetings to get organized and plan, team members may be reluctant to schedule regular meetings. They may just want to start their work instead of meeting to discuss it. But, for most teams, it is only during regular meetings that decisions can be made that will keep the team moving forward. It is at these meetings that team members keep in touch; have an opportunity to replan, if needed; and continue to build team spirit. Even teams that work closely together on a daily basis need the organized, face-to-face team meetings to deal with many of their issues.

These meetings do not need to be long or over planned. The team leader or the meeting leader can make them brief, operational meetings with a simple agenda, such as the following:

- Action items (complete, incomplete, new)
- News and information
- Operational concerns (those that can be handled by the team in a few minutes)
- Meeting evaluation (can be conducted periodically after short meetings and after all long meetings)
- Adjourn

Other meetings can be held to deal with a single, larger issue, concern, or decision. Because this type of meeting takes plenty of time and energy, the team should focus on one issue per meeting. The team leader can allow some time at the end for the team to hold a short operational meeting, if necessary.

After the team has been in Step Five long enough to accomplish some tasks and, possibly, experience some difficulties, the team should stop and take time to review progress it is making on its goals and on its cohesiveness as a team. (Step Six describes how to do this.) Team self-evaluations are a way for the team to review how it is working together and to make mid-course corrections. The team must decide the best time to initiate such an evaluation. If the evaluation is done much before the real work has started, the team will not have enough data to evaluate. If the team waits too late to review its methods and success as a team, it will miss opportunities to make timely changes. While the team is in Step Five, it should review Step Six and determine whether and when to do a team self-evaluation. Teams generally want to do an evaluation when things are going poorly on the team, but an evaluation can also be effective when things are going well. If things are going well, it is a perfect time for the team to acknowledge it and applaud the results. Team self-evaluations can be done more than once, and probably should be done several times over the life of a team. Step Six gives further pointers on when and how to do a team self-evaluation.

Determine Task Assignments

There are several things the team will need to consider when deciding who will do what tasks. Keeping with the true sense of teamwork, it is the team members—not the team leader—who determine who will do what tasks. Tasks are generally assigned by having someone volunteer, or by having someone suggest a team member for the task. In some cases, the team may want to determine guidelines for assigning tasks. Of course, the team leader may suggest assignments, just as any other team member. Following are some suggested guidelines for determining task assignments:

First, assign tasks based on members' strengths and preferences. Some team members will naturally prefer certain tasks to others, and this helps motivate them to get the work done. Others will stand out as an ideal choice for a task because of their particular skills, experience, or access to resources.

Second, consider assigning tasks to team members so they can develop skills. For example, if only one or two members do all of the team presentations, others will not develop this valuable skill. A team usually performs better when its members are multiskilled. This way the team can function well even if one of the members is absent.

Third, capitalize on the diversity of the team members when assigning tasks. It is not always productive or creative to group people together on team tasks who have the same experiences or backgrounds. Differences of opinion and experience are healthy and give team members, who may not work well together, an opportunity to build alliances and remain open-minded.

Fourth, share or rotate less desirable tasks. Someone inevitably gets stuck with a task they did not mind doing at first, but prefers not to be responsible for it forever.

Fifth, make sure someone takes responsibility for the overall co-ordination of the team's efforts. This typically falls to the team leader, but, depending on the skills, preference, and other demands made on the team leader, he or she may not be the best person to coordinate the team. Coordination involves scheduling team meetings, distributing information throughout the team, making sure that team notes (meeting minutes) are transcribed and circulated, arranging for meeting rooms and supplies, inviting guests to meetings, and so on. Again, if coordinating the team's efforts becomes a burdensome, unpleasant chore for one person, it can be rotated or shared. Usually, no one on the team wants to do the coordinating, and the details fall through the cracks. This can slow down the team's momentum and squelch enthusiasm for being on the team. Team members will start putting other things before their commitments to the team, because they will begin to believe that it does not matter if they meet their team commitments, the team is not really pulling together as a team anyway. One suggestion is for the team to list all the things that need to be coordinated and add to that list as needed. Team members can be assigned to various items on the list, and the list should be brought to team meetings to be sure everything is covered. Every few weeks, the responsibilities for coordination can be rotated.

Review Action Items and Update the Schedule Regularly

At each team meeting—except for those called to deal with a special issue—the team will post the action items from the last meeting and go over them one by one. This will let the team know what has been done and what still remains to be done. Even action items that are not due can be given time for a status report. The person responsible for the task can give team members an update on the task. When team members see that some tasks are being completed and others are in progress, it motivates them to continue working. When, for some reason, everything bogs down, it will be difficult to stir up enthusiasm again.

The planning the team did in Step Four should have included a schedule to help the team get off to a good start. This schedule will change, however, as team members tackle the various tasks and action items are completed or change. Some tasks will take more or less time than planned; others will come up that were not part of the original plan, and these must be added to the schedule. The team schedule should be updated at every meeting to keep momentum going.

Communicate Between Meetings

People on teams are usually busy people. They leave the team meeting laden with action items and race off to another meeting where they will take on more commitments. Some members must return to their jobs, where other demands are also placed on them. Work overload is a real problem for team members, and organizations are going to have to tackle this problem eventually. Work overload causes team members to get too busy to communicate with one another between meetings and makes it difficult for teams to focus the energy necessary to achieve results. Teams need to recognize how critical it is just to touch base with other team members from time to time, and to follow up so that action items can be completed. There are times when it is highly important for a team member to contact some or all other team members. Following are some situations:

- When a team member becomes aware of a resource needed by one or more team members
- When a team member has information someone else needs
- To return a teammate's phone call, fax, e-mail, and so on
- To thank a teammate
- To ask others on the team for help
- To share resources
- To get together to prepare something for the whole team

- To pass on completed work so a teammate can begin a task
- To let the team know a deadline is going to slip and why it will
- To suggest team meeting agenda items to the team

There are other reasons, but these are obvious ones. Team communication becomes ragged when team members do not pass on information to other team members or fail to alert the team to a problem. Most people are reluctant to tell others when they cannot meet an agreed-upon deadline. But it is often helpful if we do, because by mentioning a delay or problem, team members can replan their own tasks in light of the new information.

To make the team aware of these communication guidelines, the facilitator or team leader should write them on a flip chart and present them during a team meeting. The leader should post the chart and ask the team to react. Ask the team if it needs to follow the suggested guidelines. If the team does not believe they are necessary, ask them why not and to present other guidelines for the team to use to communicate between meetings. Let the team add to and delete from the list, or create a new list of its own. This may take fifteen or twenty minutes, but it will be well worth it once the team gets busy on its tasks. This approach emphasizes that *everyone owns good team communication*, not just the team leader. In the past, the manager, supervisor, or committee chairperson was responsible for seeing that communication took place among a group. With a team approach to work, *everyone* is responsible for communicating.

Identify Problems and Address Them

As much as the team hopes things will go smoothly, they almost never do, even with careful, up-front planning. Something almost always comes up to hinder the progress of the team. Resources become scarce, people do not have time to address team issues, a change in the organization brings about confusion for the team, team members leave and new members join, team members fail to cooperate with one another, or the work the team attempts may be difficult. All of these challenges are potentially part of teamwork, and the team will undoubtedly need to deal with some of them.

The team may want to purchase a copy of a helpful book called *Tips for Teams: A Ready Reference for Solving Common Team Problems*. The book is easy to use: Just open the book to the contents pages, find the problem the team is facing, and go to that page or section. Many of the typical problems the team faces will be addressed.

An effective way to address your team's problems is to get in the habit of regularly evaluating its performance as a team and selecting one or two areas to focus on for improvement. Step Six, in the next chapter, will explain how to do this. Some teams have made leaps in performance simply by evaluating themselves and committing to make corrections.

Communicate Outside the Team

One of the dangers of teamwork is that, because of the effort and time it takes to learn to work well as a team, the team will become isolated from the rest of the world. Following are four questions your team should ask itself from time to time:

1. Who needs to be informed of what we are doing?
2. What other work, by teams or individuals, do we need to be aware of?
3. What input do we need from other teams, groups, or individuals to do our job well?
4. Do we need to coordinate our work with other teams in the organization?

The team may need to regularly inform managers or other teams of its progress, or it may need to ask questions to determine how other teams or individuals are approaching a similar or related problem. Input from others in the organization, from external customers, and from those with valuable knowledge related to the team's work is critical. The team should include key resource people in some of the team meetings, or make sure someone on the team gets their input. By doing this, the team can save a lot of time and effort and it may even spark a solution.

In some cases, the team's work will overlap with the work of another team. If this is the case, the team should meet with the other team on occasion to exchange ideas, needs, and requests. Commitments may need to be made and both teams should be clear about their expectations of one another. Needs that cannot be met should also be identified with an explanation why a particular need cannot be met. If there is conflict between teams, both teams should acknowledge it and meet with the goal to resolve it jointly. It may not be necessary or wise to have all members of two or more teams meet to work out problems. Each team can send representatives who have the necessary knowledge and experience to resolve the conflict.

When working out issues between teams, the teams should agree on a problem-solving process before tackling the problem. This will reduce potential conflict over how to approach the problem, and there will be less likelihood of confusion, frustration, and power plays.

Celebrate Team Milestones

During this period of productivity, the team should remember to stop briefly from time to time and celebrate milestones it has achieved. By acknowledging its accomplishments, the team will get energy to go forward to the next task. (See Celebrating Team Milestones in the Practical Lessons in Teamwork section of this book.)

Lessons in Teamwork

During this productivity stage, your team is continually faced with the need to come up with creative solutions. This is not surprising, because if someone had already come up with solutions, the team would not be focusing on this concern or goal. Learning to work creatively will pay off for the team in the long run. Review the Foster Team Creativity lesson included in the Practical Lessons in Teamwork section of this book.

Step Six:
Review Team Performance

Teamwork is a step-by-step process, with discovery, detours, and surprises all along the way. A healthy team takes ownership for its ongoing growth and improvement and learns to periodically evaluate itself and make corrections. A team develops to the extent that all of its members are willing to continually improve, learn, and explore better team methods. A high-performing team works to constantly improve itself by regularly examining its own methods and practices.

As the team members move through the steps of teamwork, they will undoubtedly face challenges and obstacles to the work they are trying to do as a team. To overcome these obstacles and work through the challenges, your team must regularly review its progress and performance as a team.

Some of the progress review will come naturally in Step Five as the team does it work. However, Step Five is focused on accomplishing the team's tasks. In Step Six, the team will review how well it is approaching its tasks *and* how well it is working together as a team.

By evaluating the team's performance in both the task and social dimensions of teamwork, team members will find that some of the problems they couldn't solve in earlier steps are solved by focusing on several areas of team performance.

After working with a simple evaluation tool, the team will decide what areas of its own performance need improvement and how it is going to improve in those areas. A high-performing team accepts these periodic self-evaluations as an important, natural part of teamwork. The most successful teams make it a habit to regularly review team ground rules, work habits, and cohesiveness.

Over time, the team members will learn when it is time to review their performance as a team. It makes sense not to stop the positive momentum of the team to perform an evaluation, or to evaluate the team too frequently. However, when the team's momentum has slowed down, when it faces obstacles that do not seem to be going away, or when some members of the team are complaining about how the team is functioning—all of these are indications that the team should perform a team self-evaluation.

This chapter describes a process that has worked well in teams. It is not the only way to assess the team's performance, but once the team is familiar with this method, it can branch out and try other methods or variations on this one. The method suggested here aims to do the following:

- Assess all important areas of teamwork.
- Look at the team as a whole.
- Avoid embarrassing team members.
- Avoid grading, ranking, rating, or singling out team members.
- Help all team members take ownership for the team's performance as well as its improvement.
- Foster discussion among members, rather than focus on numerical results.
- Acknowledge the team's strengths as well as areas needing improvement.
- Make teams aware of the characteristics of an effective team.
- Leave the team energized with one or two areas to focus on for improvement.
- Let the team decide what to work on and how to work on it.

Complete the Team Evaluation Form

The Team Evaluation Form reflects characteristics and practices of a high-performing, successful team. Though this is not an exhaustive list, it represents key characteristics and covers the major areas of teamwork: goals, consensus, team leadership, roles, resources, support, membership, and habits and behaviors that make teams productive and cohesive.

If your team has standards that are not represented on this form, it should add them to the form. If some of the standards on the form are not important to the team, delete them, or reword them to fit your team's needs. The organization may have an evaluation tool that it prefers to use. If so, use it and adapt it if necessary. The goal is for the team members to learn to assess themselves as a team and to continually improve their teamwork. This form is provided because often teams do not have access to a simple tool they can use. Though there are many tools on the market, many of them involve special data roll-up procedures and special training to use the form. Such tools may be appropriate at times, but the team members should accustom themselves to evaluating themselves and taking the initiative to make improvements.

Some teams and organizations prefer not to use a numerical scale, such as the 1 to 6 scale used in the form. In organizations where rating and ranking have been abused or made people uncomfortable, teams may choose to drop the numerical scale and use an agreed-upon verbal scale, such as No, Sometimes, and Always, or Needs Improvement, Satisfactory, and Outstanding. Usually, there is someone on a team who is skilled at tallying, averaging, and displaying scores so team members can get an accurate picture of the overall team responses.

What is important during the evaluation process is the discussion and decisions that follow the scoring, not the scoring itself. The objective for doing a team self-evaluation should be something like this: *To identify an area or two where we can improve our performance as a team and decide how to do it.*

The first time the Team Evaluation Form is used, the facilitator or the team leader should do the following:

1. Hand out a copy to each team member.

2. Explain that this form will help the team identify areas needing improvement and that after the initial use of the form the team may want to alter it for later use.

3. Give team members quiet time to complete the form or have them bring it completed to the next meeting.

4. Make sure everyone knows what the word *team* refers to. (Ideally, this form will be completed by the team members and leader only, and they will be evaluating their team.)

Team Evaluation Form

The word *team* in this survey refers to _____ .

	(Circle one) Evaluation Scale	
	Weak	Strong
1. The team's mission and goals are written, clear, reasonable, and motivating.	1 2 3 4 5 6	
2. Members aim for the same goals and are highly committed to the team's mission.	1 2 3 4 5 6	
3. Consensus is reached without sacrificing quality.	1 2 3 4 5 6	
4. The team's work is planned, organized, and carried out in an effective way.	1 2 3 4 5 6	
5. Team meetings are timely and productive.	1 2 3 4 5 6	
6. The team is kept well-informed about events, changes, or data that affect it.	1 2 3 4 5 6	
7. Members are clear about their individual roles on the team.	1 2 3 4 5 6	
8. The team has full responsibility for a well-defined segment of work.	1 2 3 4 5 6	
9. The team has decision authority over how its work gets done.	1 2 3 4 5 6	
10. New members are accepted, supported, and well-integrated into the team.	1 2 3 4 5 6	
11. Team members have adequate equipment, resources, and skills to accomplish team goals.	1 2 3 4 5 6	
12. The team's leadership is clear, effective, and supportive.	1 2 3 4 5 6	
13. The team's tasks are reasonable in light of members' workloads.	1 2 3 4 5 6	

		Weak				Strong	
14.	Members know each other and work closely together.	1	2	3	4	5	6
15.	Members trust one another; communication is open and unguarded.	1	2	3	4	5	6
16.	Members feel a strong sense of responsibility to help the team be successful.	1	2	3	4	5	6
17.	I feel that I am fully accepted as a member of the team.	1	2	3	4	5	6
18.	Team members actively listen to one another and strive to fully understand one another's views.	1	2	3	4	5	6
19.	The team capitalizes on each other's differences, strengths, and unique capabilities.	1	2	3	4	5	6
20.	Team members seek, give, and receive feedback from one another in a caring and constructive way.	1	2	3	4	5	6
21.	Working on this team is an enjoyable and satisfying experience.	1	2	3	4	5	6
22.	Team goals are linked to goals of the larger organization.	1	2	3	4	5	6
23.	The team and its members communicate and collaborate with other groups in the organization.	1	2	3	4	5	6
24.	The team is effective in presenting its recommendations and decisions to others in the organization.	1	2	3	4	5	6
25.	The team's recommendations and ideas are given open-minded and fair consideration by people higher in the organization.	1	2	3	4	5	6

	Weak				Strong	
26. The team periodically reviews its progress toward goals.	1	2	3	4	5	6
27. The team periodically reviews how well it is working together as a team	1	2	3	4	5	6
28. The team celebrates and recognizes significant team milestones and accomplishments.	1	2	3	4	5	6
29. The team encourages and recognizes individual, as well as team, performance.	1	2	3	4	5	6
30. The team receives encouragement and recognition from people higher in the organization.	1	2	3	4	5	6
31. Team members share successes and problems with one another.	1	2	3	4	5	6
32. Team members learn from one another.	1	2	3	4	5	6

Discuss the Results

One of the team members or the facilitator should tally the results of the evaluation. He or she should show the average response to each item, and, if the team wants, the range of responses. For example, item 1's average may be 3.8 while the range of responses were from 2 to 6. The facilitator or team member should post the results for everyone to see.

During the evaluation-results meeting, the team members should read through the results and then jot down any surprises, questions, or ideas that come to mind. After a few minutes, the facilitator or the team leader should ask people to share their observations. A skilled facilitator can help during this discussion by encouraging everyone to comment and by probing so that people will be open and thoughtful in their responses.

Ask team members what they see as the key strengths or assets of their team. List these and post them for everyone to see.

Record Ideas for Team Improvement

Once the strengths have been acknowledged, the facilitator should ask the team members what improvements they believe the team needs to make, based on the results of the evaluation. The facilitator should show the lowest scored items and allow plenty of time for discussion and differences of opinion on each one. Ask team members to voluntarily share why they rated a particular item as they did. Ask, "What happens in our team to support the need to improve in this area?" List and post answers to the question, along with the list of strengths.

Decide Immediate Actions

Next, the facilitator or the team leader should have the team members agree on which one or two areas they want to work on first. They should then decide what actions the team will take to make improvements in these selected areas. The facilitator should record the actions and people responsible (it may be everyone) for each action. These action items should be part of the agenda for the next team meeting. The items should be documented in the minutes. Continue to make them part of the agenda in future meetings, if necessary.

Review Progress

At a later meeting, the team members should determine if the team has made sufficient progress on the selected areas. The team leader should ask, "How would each person rank those areas now?" If they have improved, the team leader should ask the team members how they will maintain good performance in these areas in the future. At this time, the team may want to return to the list of improvements needed and select another one or two areas to work on.

Tips on Conducting a Team Self-Evaluation

Following are some tips on conducting a team self-evaluation.

- Only the members of the team and other invited people should be present for the evaluation discussion. The team leader should participate in the evaluation as a team member, with equal (not heavily weighted) input.

- Set aside plenty of time for discussion and minimize outside distractions.

- Allow team members several minutes of quiet time in the meeting to complete the form and, later, to study the results.

- As team members read through the results, have them write down their main reactions. Reactions could be surprises, questions, areas for improvements, strengths, and so on.

- Appoint a facilitator, who will remain neutral during the discussion, to move the discussion along and record team agreement on key points.

- Discuss team members' reactions to the results. Encourage team members to share different perspectives, but make it voluntary for them to divulge their scores.

- Record the team's ideas for improvement on a flip chart for all to see.

- Review and prioritize the list of ideas for team improvements.

- Arrange to have the list of ideas typed and distributed to the team.

- Decide what follow-up is necessary (e.g., a meeting to define actions and responsibilities, a time to review the team's progress, and so on).

Step Seven: Complete the Work

Step Seven is the most crucial step in teamwork. It is the step that all previous steps have led up to, the step that justifies the existence of your team. During Step Seven, the team completes the work it set out to do.

Target Work for Completion

To successfully complete its work as a team, your team must keep the original goals in mind and stick to the plan it created. Teams may define their completed work in different ways. For some teams, the completed work may be one project among several that the team is working on; One project gets done, while others remain unfinished. Another team may work on only one project that has a beginning, a middle, and an end. This project may be the only reason the team was created. In this case, the finished work will also signify the end of the team. Other teams may be working on fragments of larger projects, projects which may involve several teams. These teams may complete work by finishing one segment and handing the project off to another team. Ongoing work teams and staff teams will complete some goals, while others may still be in the infant stage. Their goals may be the intermediate goals for the company and will be linked to the goals of other teams.

No matter whether the team has multiple projects or goals, or one single project or goal, it must aim to complete portions or all of its work. At some point in time, for a team to be successful, it must complete its work. *Teams who do not complete work are not achieving results as a team.*

Several things must happen for the team to know it has completed a portion, or all, of its work. First, the desired results or goals must have been spelled out in the beginning (either the beginning of the team or at the beginning of this period in the team's life). The desired results should have become part of the written team charter (Step One). Second, the team should have applied actions and reviewed progress toward these goals. Third, the team must come to the decision or agreement that a goal has been achieved and that the work, or at least that segment of the work, has been done. Fourth, the team should document what it has done. In Steps Eight and Nine, the team publishes its accomplishments to those outside the team who need to know the information and the team celebrates its achievement.

Look at Two Kinds of Results

Every team achieves two kinds of results: (1) process results, *how* it functioned as a team; and (2) product results, *what* it produced as a team. When the team arrives at Step Seven, it will need to document both process and product results, because in order to have completed work as a team, the team had to have had process results as well. Those outside the team, however, will be mostly interested in the team's product results: What the team did, achieved, decided, produced, or delivered as a team. People outside of the team want to see the results of the team's labors. The team needs to recognize the dual effort and take pride in both the process and product of its work.

Overcome Problems in Completing the Work

Two tendencies cause problems for teams: (1) the tendency for the team's work to drag out beyond its optimum time for completion, and (2) the tendency for organizations to impose unrealistic time pressures on a team to complete its work.

Some teams have a difficult time completing their work because several things can get in the way. If the team's original results or goals have been described inadequately, the team will have difficulty knowing when their work is done. To correct this, the team may have to rewrite its goals more clearly. After working on the project for a while, team members may have expanded the original goal and created more work for themselves. This may simply be due to oversight, it may be due to ever-growing organizational needs and demands, or it might be due to an underlying need to preserve the work, which in turn preserves jobs in a work environment where people's jobs are insecure. Sometimes team members try to perfect their work, not being content to deliver anything less than a stunning piece of work to their organization. Team members can become stymied by the problem, or become locked in disagreement over what the solution or next steps should be. The team may arrive at a good decision, but fearing the reaction the organization will have to it, keep working the decision to make it more palatable. Sometimes a team is told to go back and rework its decision, because the decision was not the decision the organization wanted. Many things can slow down the completion of a team's work.

On the other hand, some teams are given assignments that are impossible to complete in the amount of time given. When this is the case, a team feels rushed and stressed to get its work done in record time and runs into one hurdle after another due to unrealistic time pressures. When a team is not given enough time to work on a project, it does not have enough time to work as a team to define goals and strategies or to develop as a team. In such cases, a few action-oriented team members may dominate and take over the work of the team, or the team may come up with a quick, pat solution. The synergy and cooperation needed for effective teamwork will not be realized. Team members may leave the team feeling burned out or frustrated with "teamwork" and may not look forward to the next team effort. Occasionally, a team that is pushed beyond realistic demands will pull off a heroic achievement to everyone's amazement, including its own. However, it is rare for this to happen again and again, because team members cannot keep up with such a demanding pace indefinitely. Organizations need to understand that for teams to achieve results on a continuous basis, they need the time to get through Steps One through Six before reaching Step Seven.

Document What Has Been Done

Step Seven is not completed until the team has documented what it has done. The team records what it has done in relation to what was set forth in its team charter.

Once the work and documentation is complete, the team is ready to move on to the wrapping up phase of teamwork, Steps Eight, Nine, and Ten.

Phase III: Wrapping Up

Once your team's main work is completed, there is some important wrapping up to do. Wrapping up is a time for the team to stop and reflect on what has been achieved and a time to determine what the new direction will be. Project teams, whose work as a team is finished, need to officially disband so team members can move on to other work or join other teams. A project team that plans to stay together should mark the ending of one project before taking on another. To avoid getting lost in the chaotic (or humdrum) nature of their work, ongoing work teams need to pause when goals have been reached so they can summarize past successes and begin anew. The wrapping up time does not need to be dragged out, but it should not be glossed over either.

Wrapping up a team's current work, or its time together as a time, is an important milestone in teamwork. When teams fail to wrap up their work, they lose a sense of "team," and team members are left with a sense of loss. A brief period of summary, conclusion, and looking back allows the team to recognize and give credit to its achievements. For example, the team may have completed its work only after tremendous effort and sacrifice on the part of every team member. Members may be tired, burned out, elated, or just ready to get on with their next assignment. Going through Steps Eight, Nine, and Ten will bring the team to a sense of completion and prepare them for what lies ahead.

Steps Eight, Nine, and Ten also help the organization receive the most benefit from the work of the team. Results are published (Step Eight), the organization rewards and recognizes the team (Step Nine), and the team is clearly either disbanded or poised to begin its next effort (Step 10). The rituals of concluding the team's work are as important as those it followed to start up the team.

Step Eight:
Publish the Results

The team is now ready to formally let people outside the team know what it has done. If your team has communicated outside the team all along, what it has done will not be a surprise to anyone. However, the team must report in a summarized and clear manner what it accomplished. This shows the organization that the team produced the deliverable, or the end product, identified in its team charter. The report also helps to dispel any rumors or misunderstandings that may have developed concerning the team's project.

The end product need not take the form of a report or presentation, although it may. The end product may have been the successful implementation of a project, an event, or a decision. Whatever type of result the team produced, it should back up its work to the organization by publishing what it has done in the form of a written report or presentation. This does not have to be a long document or a detailed presentation of every step the team took. In fact, it should not be either of these. Instead, the team members should create a clear and brief presentation along with a handout (report) that people can read quickly and easily.

The goal of the report is to let the organization know what results were achieved and what the impact is on the organization. To carry out what the team has started usually requires support from others in the organization, and publishing the team's results is an opportunity to gain this needed support. In the report the team can provide others with information about a new process or procedure it developed, or the team can explain its actions or answer questions.

Set the Communication Goals

The type of communication the team needs to make will depend on what needs to be communicated to the organization. The team should hold a brief team meeting to determine what the team wants to accomplish when it publishes the results of its efforts. Your team may want to consider some of the following points as it writes its report:

- *Clarify* what the team has done.
- *Explain how* the team reached its decision or accomplished its results.
- *Convince people* why the team's results should be taken seriously.
- *Get support* for implementation or the next phase of work.
- *Provide key information* to people who will be affected by the team's work.
- *Help other teams* who will carry on where the team left off.
- *Persuade people* to act on the information or results of the team's efforts.

Analyze the Communication Situation

To determine what format and avenue to use to publish the team's results, the team should address the following questions:

- Who needs to be informed of the team's results (e.g., managers, team sponsors, external customers, internal customers, support organizations—such as finance or personnel, other teams, and so on)?
- What key information does each group need to be well-informed and to ensure support of the team's work?

- Which of these groups will need a chance to ask questions of the team?

- Which will simply need to know the results of the team's work?

- Given what each group needs to know and given the environment, what is the best timing and format for the team's communications?

- How can the team use its team members' skills to the best advantage when communicating these results?

Plan the Communication

The team is well-acquainted with planning by now, so this step should be straightforward. Based on the answers they came up with to the previous questions, the team should decide and plan how it will publish the results of its work. The team may choose to make small presentations to select groups, make a single presentation to a large group, write and circulate a report, or create a colorful brochure. The team will then need to decide how it will both create and deliver the communication. The team will need to answer the following questions: Who will design the presentation or write the report/brochure? Will the whole team be involved? How? What time constraints is the team under? What is its deadline for delivering the communication? Who should hear the results first? Who will actually deliver the presentations? Who outside the team needs to be informed and involved as the team plans this process?

Develop and Present the Communication

As the team develops and presents its communication, the team should aim for the following:

- Keep your communication goals in mind.

- Keep your communication clear, simple, brief, and as entertaining as possible. Present what is relevant to your *listeners*— not what is relevant to the team.

- Show the positive impact of the team's efforts on the organization.

- Anticipate questions and be prepared for them ahead of time. If the communication is written, cover anticipated questions in the material.

- Edit and/or practice your communication to accomplish your communication goals, but don't agonize over perfection. Be confident, allow for mistakes, and remain flexible. Talk (or write) to the listeners in a straightforward, personal manner.

- Make sure people know about your communication, when it is, what it will cover, what it is about.

- Determine a time and place to communicate that gives your communication every advantage.

- Avoid putting the team down or making excuses.

- Expect some skeptics or judgmental listeners, but don't take offense. Simply explain what your team set out to do and what it has done. Listen and acknowledge comments. If the team has overlooked something, admit the mistake and move on. Focus on the positive results.

Step Nine:
Reward the Team

It is now time to reward the team for its success and for the team to celebrate and acknowledge the ending point in its life as a team, or the ending point in this portion of the team's work. Your team's first reward is actually the completion of its work and the pride that this generates. This is an important, intrinsic reward.

There are also extrinsic rewards, and they can be divided into two types: internal and external. *Internal rewards* are given to the team from itself. An effective team learns to reward itself with celebrations and rituals along the way to mark both the team's milestones and the final completion of the team's work, if the team is disbanding (see "Celebrating Team Milestones" in the Practical Lessons in Teamwork section of this book). If the team has followed the previous eight steps, it will have been rewarding itself for completing important milestones.

External rewards come from outside the team when someone inside or outside the team's organization recognizes the successful performance of the team. Few individuals or teams continue to operate at maximum levels of performance without recognition from their organization. It is important that both the team and the organization come up with ways to reward successful team performance.

Recognize the Team in the Organization

One of the most powerful, and often overlooked, ways to reward a successful team in the organization is to implement its plan, adopt its decision, or heed its recommendation. These actions support the team's work, acknowledge the quality of the team's efforts, and build credibility for teams throughout the entire organization. When one or more of the following happens, the team will be deflated, and definitely not rewarded:

- The team's decision or recommendation is tabled until it can be considered by upper management.
- Someone challenges the team's work and the team must reconvene to defend its position.
- Changes in the organization make the team's work obsolete or unable to be implemented.
- Another team, or individual, has come up with a solution or recommendation to the same problem, unknown to the team.

To avoid having the team's work go unsupported in the organization, the team must do some initial work to clarify the team's boundaries. While the team is doing its work, the team needs to communicate to the organization to keep people informed and to build support for what it is doing. Once the team's work is completed, the organization should be prepared to accept and implement the decisions of the team and to publicly recognize the team's achievements. This not only rewards the team for its success, but it encourages other teams that may be struggling or getting started. When teams know they will be recognized for the work they have done, they are more motivated to work through the inevitable ups and downs of teamwork.

Therefore, one of the key responsibilities of organizational leaders who expect to get work done through teams is to devise ways to adequately recognize and reward the work done by teams.

Much work still remains to be done in the area of team rewards, and some organizations are just beginning to put systems in place to measure and reward team performance, in addition to individual performance.

Step Ten:
Move On

Once your team's charter is completed, the team and/or others in the organization will have to decide whether to disband the team or keep it going. If the team is an ongoing work group, it will reach Step Ten when it has either completed significant goals or reached the end of a set time period, such as a quarter or a year. At this point, the team will need to regroup in some way or to review and revise its goals. Certain types of teams will not disband when their work is complete, but will instead restructure themselves, perhaps starting another project, or revising their charter to carry out another aspect of the work they have completed.

It can be difficult to tell when the team's work is done. Either the team members or people outside the team come up with more work that the team needs to do. Sometimes the team members doubt the validity of their work, or management challenges the data. Finishing up the team's work can be deciding when a painting is finished. Just when you think the work is finished, you see something is not quite right. A touch of green is needed here, some blue there.

All teams come to a point where they must move on. Either the work is done, or it cannot be done, or the situation has changed so dramatically that the team must regroup. Sometimes the team, especially ongoing work teams, simply must stop and rest, and later refuel.

There are essentially three ways the team can move on. They are as follows:

1. *Disband*—The members no longer work together as a team.
2. *Restructure*—Set new team goals and rewrite the team charter, perhaps even alter team membership.
3. *Renew*—Review and revise existing team goals and its charter (this is typical for ongoing work teams or standing teams).

Each of the three options is described in the following sections.

Disband the Team

If your team no longer has results that it must achieve, it is time for it to disband. There are several reasons for disbanding the team:

- The team has successfully completed its work. Nothing more needs to be done; no follow-up is required.
- Another team (or individual) will carry on where the team left off. Hopefully, the team has handed the project, product, or service over to this other team (or individual) with adequate information and training for it to carry on successfully.
- For reasons beyond the team's control, such as budget cuts, company reorganization, redundancy with another project, the team's project/work has been stopped before completion.
- The team has requested its project/work be stopped. This may be due to inadequate resources, time, or information.
- Higher priority projects/work have taken precedence over the team's work, and team members' time and services are required elsewhere. Team members, the team leader, the team sponsor, and other managers in the organization should all be involved in the decision to disband the team.

Restructure the Team

For various reasons, it may not make sense for your team to disband, even if it has completed its team charter. The team may simply need to restructure. There may be a significant change in the focus of the team, in the team's membership or leadership, or in the group the team is serving. Organizational changes may be driving a re-organization of the team.

When significant changes must be made in a team, the team cannot simply make a few changes and carry on as before. Significant change calls for readdressing the team charter and starting back at Step One. Because the team has successfully worked together, the initial steps of organizing and focusing the team may be easier and go more quickly than the first time the team did these steps. However, it is important not to skip the steps, because, although the team may remain somewhat intact, the work, focus, and approach may need to change dramatically. If the team used a name in the past to identify itself, it may even consider changing its name to represent the new work it is going to do. In some cases, the team name may need to stay the same. This depends on the degree of change the team faces. Revision of the team's charter may also lead to changes in team membership and even team ground rules.

Renew the Team

If the team is an ongoing work group, it may never fully complete its team charter. However, from time to time, the charter will need to be revised and the team will need to review its purpose and approach as a team. All systems tend to wind down over time and need renewal. Teams are no different. It is not realistic to expect a team to continue working well together for an indefinite period of time without some effort to reassess its goals and purpose, or to change the way it is working. The growth and development of a team requires attention to the team process all along. "Growth is a spiral process, doubling back on itself, reassessing and regrouping."[1]

[1]Julia Cameron, *The Artist's Way* (New York: Putnam's Sons, 1992).

Healthy teams realize the need to spiral back, to integrate past efforts with new efforts, and, in some cases, to start over in order to benefit from lessons learned. Healthy teams learn to celebrate past victories, move beyond blocks and obstacles, and move forward with renewed commitment.

Often, when a team is lagging or in trouble, the sponsor or the team lead may call in an outside consultant or facilitator to lead a team-building session. The goals of these sessions vary from identifying the team's purpose, to setting team goals, to improving team productivity, or to finding ways to work better together. Team-building sessions can be useful in the short term to get teams back on track and to build trust and rapport among team members. However, team-building sessions do not improve the team's productivity in the long term. Teams tend to revert to the same problems unless ongoing measures are put in place that will continue the team-building benefits indefinitely. The healthiest teams learn to deal with work-related and relationship-related problems along the way. They integrate team building into the life of their team and team members and leaders take ownership for team-building efforts. Using the ten-step process outlined in this book will help the team deal with many of the typical issues addressed in a team-building session.

From time to time, the team may want to have an outside person facilitate a difficult session; but the team should not rely on team-building sessions alone to deal with its difficult issues. The healthiest, high-performing teams find ways to build their team continually. A team can be compared to a car. Cars run better with regular lubrication and oil maintenance and basic checkups. Waiting until the car breaks down can be damaging to the car, is usually costly, and causes major hassles. A routinely maintained car (and team) will have fewer, costly breakdowns.

To renew your team, members should go back to the team's original team charter and ask the following questions:

- What parts of our charter do we need to keep?
- What parts need to be revised or thrown away?

- What will we do differently based on what we have already learned about working together as a team?

- What are our team's unique strengths and how can we better capitalize on them?

- What are our team's unique weaknesses and how can we compensate for them?

- What organizational changes must we consider as we revise our charter?

It is wise for an ongoing team to include teamwork goals in their charter, as well as work goals. Teamwork goals define what type of team the members want to be. It also helps the team determine which goals it wants to set that focus on how the team works together. The team should make sure these goals support its work-related goals. Following are some teamwork goals your team might consider:

- Build team leadership skills and experience in all team members.

- Get training in problem solving and apply it.

- Identify key milestones and deadlines and celebrate when we achieve those milestones—on time.

- Establish guidelines for how we will communicate/keep informed as a team.

- Involve all team members in the selection of new members.

How to Move On

Whether it is disbanding, restructuring, or going through renewal, your team will be going through a transition. The team leader or a facilitator can help team members move smoothly through this transition by using the following guidelines.

First, do not make the mistake of stopping all team activity when the team has published its results and celebrated. If your team is disbanding, it will need a chance for members to conclude their team relationships and to pause for a chance to officially end the team. If this is not done, members may feel a sense of letdown due to incomplete work. A good time to officially end the team is after the final celebration, preferably during a short, separate meeting. Some of the things that can be accomplished are as follows:

- Team members can exchange phone numbers and addresses for future reference.

- Each team member can tell the team what he or she found most important about the team's work and about being a team. This gives members a chance to express appreciation to one another and to the team leader, and to hear others' comments.

- Make documentation available to team members for future reference, or return original copies of documentation to the originators.

- List follow-up work that needs to be done to round off the work of the team.

- Suggest the members plan a "reunion," if they want to. This might be appropriate for project teams that have completed an intense period of work together, especially if the project will have an effect beyond the life of the team. Members can reunite and renew friendships and receive updates on the progress of their project.

This meeting should be a private meeting of the team, with no guests present. Those outside the team who wish to give special recognition to the team can be invited to do this during the team celebration or at a prior meeting.

The meeting does not need to be long and drawn out, nor does it need to be emotional or dramatic in tone. The team leader or facilitator should let the team members set the tone for the meeting. The atmosphere of the meeting will depend on the success of the team and its relationships. However, even if the team struggled and there is still tension or difficulties on the team, it is a good idea to give everyone a chance at the end to clear the air. If this happens, great. If not, the team leader has at least made an effort to end the team on a positive note. When a team has been successful in its work and has grown together as a team, there will generally be a note of pride and optimism in the air at the last meeting, and in some cases, sadness or regret that the team members will not continue to work together on the same team.

If your team is restructuring or renewing, it makes sense to give the team a brief break from its meetings and its work, if possible, before jumping into the next phase of the team's work. The team leader should set aside a special meeting at which the goal is to either restructure or renew the team, and make this goal and its supporting agenda clear to the team up front, before the meeting. This way people will come to the meeting mentally prepared to tackle their new assignment.

Conclusion

Each of the ten steps to achieving team results is important. The steps are an essential part of the team journey from inception through completion of work to moving on. However, the steps are simply processes, or tools, your team will use in becoming a team and performing well as a team. The end goal is not to perform the steps. The end goal is to perform as a team. By producing well as a team, the team is making a positive impact on the team's organization.

Just as the ten steps are important, being a good team is also important. But being a good team is not the primary goal or focus: performance is. Teams are simply a vehicle for performance. They are not the solution to all of an organization's current or future needs, but they can be a marvelous tool and can be the only way to get something done. Disciplined, well-developed teams can out-perform a collection of individuals, and, in most organizations, teamwork is critical to success.

As laudable as teamwork is, however, there will always be problems in teamwork, just as there are problems in other approaches.

Learning to work as a team takes time; becoming an effective team leader or team member requires that people work differently than most people are used to working in today's organizations. New skills and knowledge are required. Organizational systems must bend and perhaps even go through major overhaul. Moving to a team approach in any organization requires effort, planning, and change on the part of all involved.

Once teamwork has been accepted in an organization, and even if organizational systems have been set up to support teams, people still must come together and become productive as a team. This takes time, learning, and focused application of resources. People may get discouraged and blame the lack of success on teams. Usually the lack of success can be blamed on factors more specific than teams, such as poor planning, lack of training, feeble support, inadequate resources, subtle sabotage (by those who are not in favor of teams), or a lack of patience during the transition to a team-based approach.

Through all of these challenges and difficulties, organizations moving to teams should remember that teams are not an end in themselves, teamwork is not a magic cure-all that will save them from downfall, and teamwork will not necessarily project them to new heights of performance. Teams are *a means to an end*, and, like any other strategy or organizational change, should be integrated into the culture with patience, foresight, planning, and a willingness to keep trying even when problems arise.

Finally, your team is a vehicle for improved performance and results in the organization. I hope the Ten Steps and the Practical Lessons in Teamwork presented in this book will be a great help to your team as it takes on the challenges of working together to produce results. May you celebrate many milestones reached. May you accomplish your team goals. And may each team member receive personal satisfaction from having been a part of a team success. Good luck on your journey.

Practical Lessons in Teamwork

As the team progresses through the ten steps to achieve results, there are lessons that, if learned along the way, will greatly benefit the team. Following are the lessons the team should review and discuss as it develops into a team:

- Making team decisions
- Holding productive team meetings
- Capitalizing on team diversity
- Understanding group dynamics
- Celebrating team milestones
- Fostering team creativity

Making Team Decisions

From the moment the team begins working together, the team will be making a lot of decisions as a team. If the team becomes a productive team that capitalizes on everyone's knowledge and experience, many, though probably not all, of its decisions will be made by consensus. The team will realize many benefits to consensus decisions. Overall, teams that are skilled in consensus decision making operate more creatively, productively, and competitively.

> In seeking mutual agreement, the consensus process fosters individual differences, personal self-reliance and self-esteem, creativity and innovation, cooperative attitudes, improved interpersonal communications and relationships, responsibility, and accountability.[1]

Sometimes the team will need to decide what type of decision is appropriate in a given situation, because not all of its decisions need to be made by consensus. It is important that each team member understand what types of decisions there are and what a consensus decision is.

---

[1]S. Saint and J. R. Lawson, *Rules for Reaching Consensus: A Modern Approach to Decision Making* (San Francisco: Pfeiffer, 1994). Copyright ©1994 by Pfeiffer, an imprint of Jossey-Bass Publishers.

Types of Decisions

The four basic types of decisions are as follows:

1. A minority decision
2. A majority decision
3. A unanimous decision
4. A consensus decision

A *minority decision* is made by one or a few team members. A minority decision may need to be made when:

- There is no time to draw everyone into the process;
- Only a few people are affected by the decision; or
- The team assigned the decision responsibility to one or a few team members.

A minority decision may be used when only a few team members have the expertise needed to make the decision, when it is more time-efficient to parcel out the decision making, or when the size of the team is unwieldy for the decision that needs to be made.

The advantages of a minority decision are that it is quick and efficient and capitalizes on certain members' skills or knowledge. For example, if the team needs to make a highly technical decision, it should allow those on the team who are technical experts to make the decision. The rest of the team can be involved in setting criteria, boundaries, and guidelines for the decision and giving input along the way, while the sub-team makes the final decision. When a minority decision is made by a high-performing team, however, the sub-team that made the decision generally brings the decision in the form of a recommendation to the team, and the team makes the true final decision. This process ensures that there will be a high commitment to the decision by all team members.

The main disadvantage to minority decisions is that the team's commitment to the decision may not be strong enough to implement it, and the quality of the decision may suffer because of insufficient diversity of input. If members of the sub-team think too much alike, important decision factors may be overlooked. Generally speaking, even a technical decision warrants input and feedback from those who will be affected by the decision.

Note: The team leader or the facilitator should make sure team members are not absolving themselves of responsibility or difficulty by letting someone else make the decision. Team members must fully support the decisions they delegate to someone else.

A *majority decision* is made by a simple vote. The decision with the most support "wins." In majority decisions, there are always some people who "lose," and, depending on the strength of their views and the emotional stake they had in the outcome, "the losers" may be disgruntled and resist fully supporting the decision. Worse yet, they may resent those who supported the decision, which could cause dissension in the team. This not only affects that particular decision, but it makes further cooperative efforts on the team difficult.

The advantages of a majority decision are as follows:

- It is quick and efficient.
- It works well for decisions that will not affect the long-term progress or spirit of the team.
- It works well for relatively unimportant decisions that require little support for implementation and will not create hard feelings.

A *unanimous decision* occurs when the whole team agrees on one alternative. The main advantage of unanimous agreement is the commitment that usually follows. Disadvantages to a unanimous decision are as follows:

- Quick, unanimous agreement may lead to a poor decision.
- The phenomenon of group think may be at work. *Group think* is the tendency for team members to place high priority on agreeing with one another. A team caught up in group think

is, or wants to be, so harmonious and united that it moves quickly to agreement without carefully considering alternate views or the possible negative impact of its decisions.

- A drawn-out, unanimous decision may occur when people give in and agree to the decision because they want to end a lengthy discussion and to get the decision made. In this case, commitment to the decision may be low and viable options overlooked.

Team members are often confused about consensus. Some think it means everyone must agree with everyone else. The members may be apprehensive about being expected to achieve consensus, especially on topics and issues of long-standing concern and disagreement.

Consensus means general agreement. Reaching consensus is the act of gaining general agreement so that everyone can fully support the decision. It is a win-win solution in which everyone feels he or she has "won" without having to give in on strongly held beliefs, opinions, or ideas. In their book *Rules for Reaching Consensus*, authors Saint and Lawson define consensus as follows:

A state of mutual agreement among members of a group where all legitimate concerns of individuals have been addressed to the satisfaction of the group.[2]

Reaching consensus is different from negotiating. The two methods of arriving at a decision are quite different. In a negotiation, two or more parties present their stance, or solution, and compromises are made along the way by the parties to come to a mutually workable solution. In a negotiation, it is common for all parties involved to trade one desirable outcome for another. However, a consensus decision is reached when group members share goals, needs,

---

[2]Saint and Lawson, *Rules for Reaching Consensus*.

ideas, and concerns, and through the process of discussing, evaluating, gathering information, debating, organizing, and prioritizing, they create a solution together. Both decisions arrive at general agreement, but the consensus process is apt to reach a more creative solution and result in a higher level of commitment to the decision. It is also a less adversarial process, and, although conflict may occur during consensus decision making, it is generally healthier than the type of conflict that occurs during a negotiation.

The disadvantages to consensus decisions are that it takes time and patience, and, in the case of difficult, complex decisions, requires someone with good facilitation skills to guide the team through an appropriate decision process. Therefore, consensus should be reserved for important decisions that require a high degree of support from those who will implement them. Although it often seems time-consuming and frustrating to reach consensus, it is far more effective than disregarding the concerns and alternative ideas of other team members.

Consensus Is Not

- Voting
- A win-lose situation
- Compromising (a settlement of differences by mutually giving in)
- Dictating the conclusion
- Everyone agreeing on every point
- Forced unanimity
- Suppression of minority views and dissent

Consensus Is

- A point of maximum agreement so action can follow
- A win-win solution

- A decision everyone can support
- Creative collaboration
- A team effort to achieve an agreed-upon team goal

How to Reach Consensus

There are several ways a team leader or a facilitator can help the team work productively toward consensus. Following are some of them:

- Allow plenty of time. Sometimes, the team may need several meetings to make a consensus decision.
- Use rational, structured methods, such as brainstorming, decision matrix, problem solving, nominal group technique, list reduction, and so on. (A good resource that describes how to use various consensus tools is *The Quality Toolbox*, by Nancy R. Tague, ASQC Quality Press.)
- Check with the team before you move on. Consensus will need to be reached at several points in the process before moving on.
- Write out what was decided and post it for all to see. This will clarify what the team has agreed to, provide a decision record, motivate individuals to keep the agreement, and maintain team members' energy and attention.
- Help the team avoid group think by asking questions to stimulate creative thinking. Are there other alternatives we should consider? What are we overlooking? Have we considered all the consequences?

How Team Members Can Help Reach Consensus

One of the team members' responsibilities is to help the team reach consensus in a creative, productive way. The goal is not to avoid conflict (there should be healthy conflict) but to work through the conflict to arrive at the best solution possible. Team members need to remember "they are working cooperatively to make the best decision in support of the purposes, goals, values, and mission of the organization."[3] Effective team members strive to be consensus seekers.

> Consensus seekers understand that the only way to truly win, to get what they want and to keep it, is to make sure all parties involved also get what they want. To make the approach work, all parties have to recognize this practicality and be genuinely concerned that all parties' needs are met, though never at the expense of the other.[4]

Here's how members can be consensus seekers and help the team reach consensus:

- Avoid arguing for your own solution.
- Give full attention to the team members.
- Ask questions to make sure you understand others' main points.
- Clarify your understanding of another's viewpoint by stating their views back to them, without criticizing.
- Find merit in the other person's view.
- Avoid interrupting or defending your own ideas until you have understood what the other person has said.
- When interrupted, kindly ask people to let you finish making your points. You can say, "Please, I'd like to finish making my point."
- Do not hold back when you disagree or have another idea.

---

[3]Saint and Lawson, *Rules for Reaching Consensus*.

[4]D. A. Tagliere, *How to Meet, Think, and Work to Consensus* (San Francisco: Pfeiffer, 1992). Copyright ©1992 by Pfeiffer, an imprint of Jossey-Bass Publishers.

- Do not agree or change your mind just to avoid conflict. Instead, state your own ideas clearly, firmly, and without being overly emotional.

- Once you have made your point, avoid harping on it. Let your idea stand on its own merit.

- Aim for the expression of a lot of ideas. Build on other people's ideas.

- Draw out quieter team members by asking them what they think.

- Use differences of opinion as an opportunity for creativity rather than a hindrance to decision making.

- Avoid jumping to solutions when there appears to be initial agreement. Instead, ask questions to keep people thinking of alternatives. Discuss the reasons for agreement and determine if other viable possibilities have been overlooked.

- Try not to get personally invested in your own position. Keep the end goal in mind, and do not take it personally if the team decides to take another approach.

- Do not stall the process. Offer suggestions instead of simply disagreeing or criticizing someone else's approach.

- Support only those solutions you can live with.

- Keep the end goal in mind, which is to reach a mutually agreeable solution that will satisfy as much of everyone's needs as possible.

When team members learn these skills, the conflict that naturally occurs in teamwork is likely to be more focused on the content of the decision, which is healthy, and less focused on interpersonal differences and lack of good team communication skills. In fact, teams need these skills to work through conflict. The goal is not to avoid conflict completely, but to avoid unproductive behaviors that create more conflict or keep the team from making progress.

A Consensus Decision Process

There are basically six steps to making a consensus decision:

1. *Set the decision goal.* The team should determine what is the purpose of its decision. For example, if the team is choosing software that it will use in a network fashion, its decision goal may be to select the software package that will make the team members productive as a team. Without an agreed-upon goal, constructive consensus will be impossible. Indeed, the team's first consensus decision may be to determine the end goal.

2. *Spell out the criteria that will make the team's decision a good one.* List the qualities or characteristics the decision needs to satisfy the team's goal. This will include budget constraints, what the decision will provide the team, and what quality standards the decision must meet. The team can further help the decision process if it distinguishes between what criteria the team's decision *must meet* and what criteria is *desirable,* but not essential.

3. *Gather information.* Team members should concentrate on information the team needs to determine the best decision.

4. *Brainstorm possible options or solutions.* The team leader or the facilitator should make sure everyone understands the meaning of each option before moving on to the next step.

5. *Evaluate the brainstormed options against the team's criteria.* The team should discuss options that appear most likely to meet its criteria and then evaluate how well they actually do meet the team's list of criteria. Any viable option will have to meet all of the team's "must have" criteria. The team may want to use a decision matrix to do this. First, one of the members lists the criteria on the vertical column and then lists the options across the top, horizontally. He or she indicates which are the "must have" criteria. Then the member checks if each option

meets the "must have" criteria. Eliminate any that do not. The team can then evaluate how well each of the remaining options meet the "desirable" criteria. The member can use a numerical scale (for example, 1 to 5) to help the team decide which options come out stronger than others. The option that best meets the team's criteria, and thus the team's decision goal, will more than likely be the best choice. If none of the options meets the team's criteria, the team will need to either revise its criteria or seek more options. The team might be able to combine, or alter, options until they fit its criteria.

6. *Make the decision as a team.* The team should be sure to check for full consensus before assuming that everyone supports the decision. If someone has reservations, the team should discuss why and try to come up with a way to alleviate or eliminate those concerns.

A participant in a consensus workshop pointed out that consensus is as simple as A-B-C: Address the issue (steps 1 to 3 for making a consensus decision), Brainstorm the alternatives (steps 4 and 5), Come to consensus (the final step). Indeed, sometimes it can be that simple.

How to Recognize Group Think

Participants in my workshops sometimes ask me, "How do we know when we are operating in a group-think mode?" Some of the symptoms of group think are as follows:

- The group is highly cohesive.
- The group believes it is invulnerable.
- As a whole, the group discounts contrary information.
- The group believes that what it wants to do is inherently moral.

- The group is insulated from other groups with different views.
- The group puts pressure on dissenters to silence them.
- The group moves forward believing that "silence means consent."
- The group lacks systematic methods for evaluating alternatives.
- The group has strong, directive leaders who discourage dissent.
- The group is under high stress to come up with a quick solution.[5]

[5]Schein, Edgar H., ORGANIZATIONAL PSYCHOLOGY, 3/e, © 1980, pp. 169, 170. Adapted by Permission of Prentice Hall, Upper Saddle River, NJ.

Holding Productive
Team Meetings

"Meetings are at the very heart of teamwork because of the important functions meetings perform. Much of what gets done in teams has a foundation in the group meeting."[1] If the team is going to perform well, it must hold regular, productive, and efficient meetings.

> Meetings are often the only time the team or group actually exists and works as a group. . . . In meetings, the team's goals, direction, and norms for operating are established. Meetings create in all present a commitment to the decisions that the group makes and the objectives that the group pursues. Meetings are the forum for gaining consensus, solving group problems, and making group decisions. . . . It is in the meeting setting where much information is shared, complexities are dealt with, misunderstandings are clarified, cross-functional issues and views are aired, and vital decisions are addressed.[2]

Tips for a Productive Team Meeting

Following are some tips for having productive team meetings:

[1]Fran Rees, *How to Lead Work Teams: Facilitation Skills* (San Francisco: Pfeiffer, 1991). Copyright ©1991 by Pfeiffer, an imprint of Jossey-Bass Publishers.
[2]Rees, *How to Lead Work Teams*.

- *Plan an appropriate length of time for the meeting, not too long or too short.* The team leader should allow time for consensus, but take into account that people get tired and lose creativity after two or three hours of meeting time. A team can have a productive meeting in 30 minutes, or one hour, depending on the nature of the meeting.

- *Notify everyone of the meeting.* The team leader should make sure everyone knows the meeting date, place, times, and purpose. Notify the members so that they have time to plan for the meeting and that they know what to bring to the meeting.

- *Start and end on time.* The meeting facilitator should leave at least 15 minutes at the end of the meeting for wrap-up: time to evaluate the meeting; discuss the next meeting time, date, place, and purpose; and for team members to converse one-on-one if necessary.

- *Make sure someone facilitates the meeting.* The team may not always have an outside facilitator, but someone who has facilitation skills and can play the facilitator role should lead the meeting.

- *Have adequate tools, supplies, and documentation on hand.* Much time can be saved this way.

- *Post clear, results-oriented objectives to focus the meeting.* The team leader or facilitator should go over these at the beginning, and check to see that everyone agrees to these objectives.

- *Post the team's mission and ground rules.* Review them briefly and use them to focus the team when it gets off track.

- *Record all task assignments, decisions, and issues for future meetings.* When doing this, the team leader or the recorder should be sure to include who is responsible for each task and the target date for completion. The leader should check for agreement among all team members on the actions and decisions the team agreed to. For efficiency, the team leader or facilitator should hang several flip charts on the walls ahead of time. Use the following headings for each chart: Decisions Made Today, Issues for Future Meetings, Task Assignments (or Action Items).

- *Ask team members to help decide the objectives and agenda for the next meeting.* Highly productive teams will become skilled at determining the results they need to achieve at their upcoming team meetings.

- *Stay focused on the stated objectives for the meeting.* The team leader or the facilitator should make sure team members leave the meeting having accomplished something. If the original objectives cannot be met, restate them during the meeting so they can be.

- *Set the next meeting date and time, if possible.*

For lengthy meetings (three hours or more), it helps to have an introductory icebreaker to relax the team and get everyone involved. Longer meetings require breaks and the chance for people to get up and move around. Activities can be diversified, different processes used, and people broken up into sub-groups—all to vary the pace and format of the meeting. The team leader of the facilitator should leave 20 to 30 minutes at the end of a long meeting to evaluate the meeting, set the next meeting time and date, and to summarize all actions assigned and decisions made.

Team Meeting Needs

Most team meetings require basic facilities and supplies. The team leader should keep a list of the team's basic meeting needs and check it before each meeting to make sure the team will not lose productivity during the meeting because supplies are missing. Following are some basic supplies for meetings:

- A meeting room that is comfortable (not too crowded) and adequate for focused team work. A noisy room close to where team members work may create too many disruptions.

FIGURE 3 Flip Chart Pages

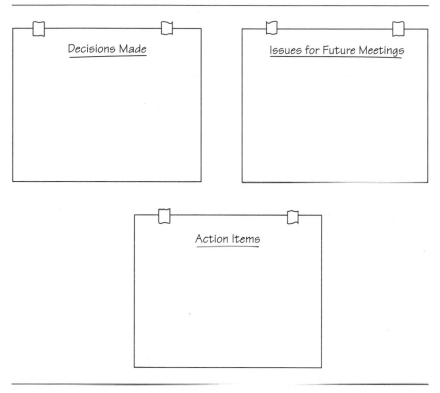

- One or two flip chart easels (or places to hang flip chart pads). White boards are too small for most team meetings.

- One or two flip chart pads. (The ones marked with light blue, one-inch grids are handy to use.)

- Several colors of waterbase marking pens. (Such pens will not bleed through to the walls when the facilitator writes on posted flip charts.)

- Masking tape for posting flip charts.

- Resource materials the team frequently uses, such as *The Quality Tool Box,* by Nancy Tague, which outlines about 50 processes teams can use to solve problems, gather data, brainstorm, prioritize, make decisions, and plan.

- Blank forms the team uses frequently, such as fishbone diagrams, action item charts, pareto charts, decision matrixes, meeting evaluation forms, and so on.
- A copy of all team documentation to date.
- Miscellaneous desk items, such as scissors, paper clips, tape, pencils, note pads, and so on.
- This book, for reference.

How to Evaluate Your Team Meeting

There are several ways to evaluate a team meeting; some of them are easier and quicker than others. Following are a few suggestions:

- *Use a quick, round-robin technique.* One of the following methods will work: (1) The facilitator or team leader asks each team member to comment briefly on the quality of the meeting. Go around the room and make sure everyone contributes. (2) The facilitator asks each person to sum up the meeting in three words. The facilitator should record the words on a flip chart. (3) The facilitator asks each person to state one thing that went well during the meeting and one thing that could be improved. (4) The facilitator asks the question, "How did our meeting go today?" and asks each person to respond briefly.
- *Use an evaluation form at the end of each meeting.* Have all the team members fill out a form. Then have someone on the team (perhaps a different person each time) take the completed forms and summarize the responses at the beginning of the next meeting. Before beginning this next meeting, the facilitator should ask the team to decide one or two things that can be improved during the meeting. Post these items and encourage people to make the improvements.

The team should periodically evaluate its meetings using the Meeting Evaluation Form on the following page, or the team can create its own form. Some teams use a much simpler form after every meeting and have each member complete it. The facilitator and team leader can use this feedback to improve the team meetings. From time to time, the team members should complete a more detailed form, such as the one at the end of the chapter, and discuss what changes they would like to make in their meetings. Both types of evaluations are useful and can be used in conjunction with the round-robin technique mentioned earlier.

Meeting Evaluation Form

Use this evaluation form as a guideline for successful team meetings and to evaluate your meetings. If necessary, modify the form to meet your needs.

	We're doing well	We need to improve
1. The meeting room and supplies are adequate for our work as a team.		
2. Members are regularly present at the team's meetings and stay through the entire meeting.		
3. We have enough—but not too many—team meetings.		
4. When members must be absent from the meeting, they find out what happened and support the decisions made.		
5. Meetings are led by someone with adequate facilitation skills.		
6. The meeting facilitator serves as a guide and does not use the position to influence the team's decision.		
7. Meetings generally start and end on time.		
8. The objectives and purpose of each meeting are clear and posted for all to see.		
9. We make good progress at our meetings.		
10. Team members listen well to one another and acknowledge the merit of one another's ideas.		

	We're doing well	We need to improve
11. Team members actively contribute to the objectives of the meeting.		
12. There is balanced participation at our meetings.		
13. Generally, we stay focused during our meetings.		
14. Action items and decisions are posted and agreed upon by those present.		
15. When there is conflict, we strive to come up with a win-win solution.		
16. We have the necessary documentation during our meetings.		
17. Team members are invited to evaluate or comment on the success of the meeting.		
18. Adequate time is allowed for consensus and to complete the meeting agenda.		
19. Ideas are accurately and objectively recorded on the flip charts.		
20. Team members use effective discussion skills during team meetings (e.g., listening, asking questions, clarifying, acknowledging other's views, expressing own ideas).		
21. Conflict is handled openly and constructively during our meetings.		
22. The flip charts are transcribed into minutes following each meeting and each member is given a copy.		

Capitalizing on Team Diversity

In today's world, teamwork and diversity go hand in hand. No matter what the makeup of a team, it can be said that any team is a collection of diverse individuals. In today's workplace, this is more true than ever.

Diversity can be one of your team's greatest assets. If not handled positively, however, it can become a block to teamwork. Most modern organizations today employ individuals from many backgrounds, walks of life, and even from countries around the world. If the team members take a moment to observe their workplace or the makeup of the team, they will notice how diverse their organization and their team is. They will find people who are different in many ways. Some will come from different ethnic, cultural, educational, and experiential backgrounds. Others will have different personalities or styles, and others will differ in gender, age, religion, and so on. There may be differences in sexual preference. In addition, there are certainly differences in work experience and seniority in the organization. The team will probably have both married and single team members and those with and without children. There will also be different feelings and thoughts about work and the workplace.

Even if your team is not particularly diverse, it will likely serve a diverse organization and a diverse customer base.

When people bring a variety of work and life experiences, viewpoints, and talents to your team, there are more opportunities for quality decision making. Most decisions made today must take into account a variety of issues, such as customers and their needs, the benefits and limits of technology, gaining support from various people or groups who will be affected by the decision, and frequently complex and confusing alternatives. Having multiple perspectives may slow the discussion down from time to time, but will usually lead to a better quality decision.

Today's organizations are collections of diverse groups and people. The challenge is to harness that diversity so that productivity is the result, not disruption and lowered productivity and quality. Following the ten steps to achieving results as a team that are outlined in this book is one way to ensure balanced involvement of everyone on the team. Teamwork is a great way to help employees learn to work across diversity in a healthy way. Working together in a team that has a focused and a clearly designated output gives people a chance to apply their diverse perspectives and backgrounds to achieve a common goal. In the close-knit manner in which teams must work, there are many opportunities to put diversity to work constructively. Once this becomes the norm, team members become less and less aware of differences, and more and more aware of unity.

Avoid Subtle Exclusion of Team Members

Some team members will ignore or gloss over a person in the group who has a different view. Sometimes team members do not want to take the time to review what might be a creative alternative. People often pre-judge or stereotype a person's ideas because that person does not appear to be part of the mainstream of the organization. The goal of healthy teamwork is to consider everyone's ideas and to depersonalize the inputs so that ideas stand on their own merit. Another goal of healthy teamwork is to build cohesiveness as a group, to become a working unit. A good team does not exclude certain members for any reason. If there are members who are simply unwilling to be a part of the team and refuse to be included, that is another matter. Subtle forms of exclusion, however, are inappropriate in teamwork. Subtle forms of exclusion may include

- Not responding to a team member's comments
- Never sitting by a team member during meetings
- Not seeking input from that team member
- Not inviting that team member to join you for a break or lunch
- Not seeking out a team member between team meetings (for short discussions, hallway chats, to work on something together, and so on)
- Not referring to that team member by name
- Not building on that team member's ideas
- Being friendly in one manner to other team members, but changing behaviors with that team member

Many organizations have included diversity awareness in their training. Some have targeted broad-sweeping organizational changes to decrease stereotyping and unfair employee practices. However, until individuals learn to be comfortable with and work productively with a diversity of people, little progress can be made. Until team members can work side by side, without stereotyping and making assumptions about one another, teams will have trouble performing.

Become Comfortable with Diversity

Effective teamwork thrives on differences among its team members and builds on that diversity. Teams should not swallow up, or ignore, individuals, but instead fully utilize individual strengths to maximize team output. In healthy teams, members can talk openly about their differences, as they apply to working and getting along together, and because of this open acceptance of difference, the members can move forward to achieve targeted results as a team. True teamwork does not let members avoid people with whom they feel uncomfortable working. True teamwork demands that the members figure out how to work with other people. Without teams, employees can avoid one another in the workplace and stay distant.

Following are some ways team members can become comfortable with the diversity of their team and capitalize on the various talents of all members:

- Do not assume the other person thinks, feels, or sees things the same way you do.

- Do not let yourself be intimidated by difference. Reach out. Try to get to know others as unique individuals. Do not be daunted if there seems to be little common ground. Honor the differences. Show interest in the person. Sooner or later, there will be common ground.

- If the other person offers information on hobbies or family, ask questions to learn more about his or her interests.

- Learn to ask open-ended questions to draw out the other person. "What is your reaction to . . . ?" "What has been your experience with . . . ?" "How do you feel about . . . ?" Avoid political, religious, or overly personal subjects initially. Concentrate on work or community-related issues.

- Find out what other people's work experience has been. Work is usually a common-ground experience for people. Remember not to focus on levels or positions in the organizations—this may push you further apart.

- Learn what others would like to get out of being on the team.

- Make it your goal to learn ways that each person is unique. For example, if a person is a member of an ethnic group other than your own, find out how he or she is different from the stereotypes of that group. If they are a member of the opposite sex, how are they unique—not just a typical man, or woman? Begin to form a personal composite of each person that is separate from his or her difference.

- Learn to dwell on ways you are similar to others on the team.
  Think of yourself and your teammates as all part of the human
  race and discover how that humanity plays out on the team.

Keep in mind this important truth:

When we look for differences, we find them.
When we seek similarities, we find those too.
The wise person searches for both, and in so doing discovers
an individual.

A few years ago, a training manager at Sematech asked me to
share some of my thoughts about diversity with her. One of her responsibilities was to review diversity training and make a recommendation to Sematech about how to proceed. There was little or
no budget slated for this type of training, but she felt it was necessary.
I gave her something I had written called the Diversity Credo—
a set of statements that, if believed and practiced by companies, I
thought would turn around the negative aspects of diversity and
help organizations deal with this issue. I have chosen to share it
here in its entirety, because I believe it speaks as well to teams.

A Diversity Credo

We believe that

- Diversity is an asset, not a liability.

- Diversity is more than tolerating difference. It is more than behaving properly. It is more than bending to meet the needs of a diverse workforce. Diversity is unrealized opportunity.

- Diversity is a business imperative. Companies cannot afford to ignore the needs, interests, and views of their most valuable asset: people. Companies need the support of all their people to succeed.

- Employees who feel understood and supported, support their companies in return. If people experience mistreatment because they are "different," they will not feel supported. Energy expended feeling unsupported is wasted energy and lowers productivity.

- Diversity training and awareness should not center on making people uncomfortable or attacking them, but it should center on understanding one another.

- Diversity trainers should offer participants a "safe haven" in which to learn, grow, express, and discover.

- On the other hand, diversity training should not ignore the real issues. Skilled trainers and well-designed programs will avoid attacking participants without watering down the issues.

- Companies that choose not to deal with diversity—do deal with it. Silence is just one way. Open discussion and measurable change is another. The silent treatment leads to resentment and lowered productivity. Openness and positive change create an atmosphere where employees more fully apply themselves, because they are valued for who they are and what they do.

Cooperation, not Competition

I see the American workplace maturing to a new level in the late century. Out of necessity, cooperation is becoming more important than competition: cooperation within the organization to get things done, cooperation with suppliers, cooperation with customers. Companies are finding that to compete effectively, they must learn cooperation and collaboration skills, that liaisons are better than enemies, and that not much gets done without a lot of folks doing their job consistently and caringly.

As technology mechanizes us and diversity confounds us, there is a growing need for communication and understanding as well as the willingness to help out one another. The cubby-hole nature of large organizations created places where people holed up and waited to talk to their boss, if and when the boss showed up. Today, these cubby-holes are being broken down as people are forced to come together more and more often to solve problems and to accomplish daily work tasks. Through teamwork, people can break down barriers to working together. In a team situation, where everyone is contributing to and influencing the team, there is less chance that people will maintain, either consciously or unconsciously, a sense of superiority. In effective teamwork, the superiority/inferiority imbalances have a chance to be equaled out. In a team, at some point, each person's needs are secondary to the whole, and at some point, each person's needs may surface and be thoroughly supported by the team. Every member gets the front seat from time to time, so that individualism feeds the synergy of the whole, and teamwork neutralizes the status games people play.

If one of your teammates seems off track, or you simply cannot relate to what he or she is saying, ask yourself: What might my teammate be saying that I am overlooking? What can I see from that person's perspective that will help me understand what is best for the team? What goal might be motivating to him or her? What can I agree with, or at least relate to, about what my teammate is saying? When have I ever felt or thought the same way, or a similar way? To sincerely answer this last question requires your ability to have empathy for another person. Empathy for another draws us closer to that person. Lack of empathy, or the unwillingness to try to relate to how another person feels or thinks, creates a distance between you and the other person. Simply recalling a time or situation in which you have had similar feelings or thoughts will help you empathize with someone else. You do not have to feel or think what they are feeling; you have to try to *relate to* what they are feeling or thinking.

Finally, remember all people are complex and can change. So do not label people, even if you think you know them. Remember to keep in touch with your teammates and their changes. Give them a broad field in which to be their changeable, growing selves, because that is what you will need from them.

Understanding Group Dynamics

The team will benefit from understanding the basic principles of what happens in groups of people, especially when they must work closely together. This area of study was labeled *group dynamics* by sociologists who attempted to discover what typically goes on in groups. After years of research on groups, sociologists found that there are no hard and fast rules for group behavior, only basic principles that tend to govern how people behave in group settings. Because a group is dynamic, ever changing, and complex, people can only estimate how group members will behave and try to predict what may happen in a group. This chapter includes some basic principles of group dynamics to help team members understand teamwork better.

Your work team is a group. A family is a group. A sports team is a group. Friends who hang out together make up a group. Even gangs are groups. Wherever a collection of individuals comes together frequently to accomplish some common declared or undeclared purpose, a group is formed. Sometimes people become inadvertently, or even unwillingly, part of a group, such as people on an airplane that is being hijacked, or parents at a little league football game. Certain generalizations can be made about groups and the behaviors people tend to have in groups. However, because of the diversity of individuals and, therefore, of the groups to which they belong, group behavior is not static, nor can it always be predicted.

As your team progresses through its work as a team, it will show some of the typical characteristics of a group, and team members will function better if they understand some of the basics of *groupness*.

Basic Principles of Group Dynamics

A *group* can be defined as a collection of two or more persons who interact with one another so as to influence and be influenced by one another. Group members can influence each other only through behaviors; that is some kind of exchange, usually communication, through which one member influences another. A group is knit together by a common goal and some kind of group structure (e.g., team, family, friendship) and is held together as a result of interdependence and interaction among the members. For a group to be successful, that is, for it to achieve its common goal, many things have to happen.

First, an interpersonal trust must develop among team members. Trust among team members only comes about over time when members have reason to believe in, and to some extent predict, the behavior of others in their group. Trust is the cornerstone in any successful team.

Next, the team must pay attention to two aspects: task and social. There is always the work (task dimension) of the team to be done and there are always the relationships (social dimension) to consider. The *task aspect* of teamwork refers to the work that the team does, such as developing, deciding, planning, acting, servicing customers, and designing systems. The social dimension is a little harder to pin down or describe. Basically, it represents how the team members relate to one another, how well they get along, how they resolve disagreements and whether everyone has an equal opportunity to contribute to and influence the team's decisions. On a deeper level, the social aspect of teamwork reflects whether all team members are valued and respected by the team leader and by the team members. Every team is a diverse collection of individuals and personalities. Therefore, every team has to work out whether and how it will value all its members. This is more difficult for some teams than it is for others.

Though the two dimensions of teamwork—the task and social—can be discussed and viewed separately, they are really inseparable. For a team to get its work done, team members must have a certain degree of mutual respect and loyalty to one another. This does not mean that members of a work team must all like one another, or that they would choose to work together if they had the choice. What it means is, over time team members build a mutual trust and respect that gives a good foundation to the social aspect of their team. Without a certain amount of respect and trust, the work of the team does not get done. On the other hand, just having trust and respect does not mean the team will get its work done. Even close teams need information, productivity tools, and other resources to accomplish their tasks. For a team to be successful, it must pay attention to both aspects of teamwork all the time. The team, like the human body, is all one system. A problem in one area can affect other areas, and strength in one area can contribute to the success of the whole.

At any point in a team's existence, the "pulse" of either of these two dimensions can be taken to determine where to put more effort. To assess the team, members should ask the following questions:

- Do we know what we are supposed to do as a team?
- Are we doing it?
- Are we doing it on a timely basis?
- Do we have a quality output?

To determine whether your team is functioning well as a team, members should ask the following questions:

- Do we have a sense of the team's mission?
- Are we putting forth energy and effort to get the work done?

- Do all team members feel valued and important to the work of the team?

- Are interpersonal relationships open and smooth enough to accomplish the team's work?

The team members should try to keep a healthy balance between tasks and team-building activities. Too much attention to the tasks may cause the team to ignore concerns of its members in the name of efficiency. When a few members take over the work of the group in the interest of time and quick progress, other members feel alienated and eventually the team becomes fractured. When a few members take over, the value of multiple perspectives and knowledge is lost, which is one of the key reasons for forming a team. On the other hand, if the team members spend too much time on interpersonal relationships, the team may turn into a social club and progress may suffer. The team should remember that the end goal is team productivity, not team spirit. However, team spirit feeds team productivity. One interesting phenomenon of teamwork is that when a team gets productive (as a whole team), team spirit follows. Another equally powerful phenomenon is that when a team fuels productivity with team spirit, productivity soars.

A third important aspect of healthy teamwork is the preservation of the individual in the team. For a group to be successful and to take advantage of synergy among its members, each team member must maintain his or her uniqueness as an individual. In other words, in a healthy group, all the members do not think, look, or act alike. Successful teams encourage a variety of viewpoints, knowledge, and experience. Diversity and conflict are valued. Conflict is treated as healthy, processes are put in place to deal with it, and team members understand that conflict is part of making quality decisions.

On the other hand, when conformity is expected, valued, and rewarded in a group, members tend to seek harmony and agreement with one another at all costs. This phenomenon is called *group think*. When group think is at work in a team, diversity of opinion is discouraged and members are pressured to conform to the opinions of others and to maintain strong in-group loyalty. Teams caught up in group think tend to believe that those outside their group are less capable and less aware than they are. Decisions made when group think is present are generally ineffective, because members have placed higher value on agreeing than on working through a variety of perspectives to consensus. In teamwork, the consideration and balance of a variety of perspectives is essential; this means honoring the difference within the group and using diversity to stimulate creativity.

Another aspect of group dynamics is that group work is often frustrating and slow. It takes time for a team to build rapport and establish a history together, which it must do before it can function effectively. Particularly in the early stages of a team's development, team members become discouraged with the amount of time it takes to make something happen and long to get on with the "real work" of the team. However, once the initial slower period of team development has taken place, a team's progress can be rapid and impressive. Team members need to expect a slow start and not get discouraged at what seems like the group's lack of progress. Patience is an important virtue in teamwork.

An important phenomenon of groups is that, when operating well as a group, they will make higher-quality decisions than individuals. In organizations today, where a decision may affect several departments or divisions, customers, and suppliers, it is critical to bring together representative perspectives. When there is adequate representation in a group, the group can reach a decision that satisfies several groups of people. The decisions being made by organizations and companies today are more complex than ever before. In many cases, decisions simply cannot be made by any one individual, because no one has the combination of knowledge, experience, and expertise required to make the decision. In still other cases, more than one perspective causes everyone to reexamine his or her original opinion, consider others' points, and come up with a better judgment. There is considerable evidence that for some types of decisions in some environments, a group will arrive at a better decision than a collection of individuals working separately. Tasks can be divided into three types:

1. Those that only an individual expert can do, such as solve a complex, mathematical equation

2. Those that can be performed equally well by an individual or a group, such as repetitive or detail work

3. Those that require group involvement or commitment for success; in such situations it is not possible to validate any single answer as the best one, but consensus is essential for implementation to succeed (An example might be how to reorganize the department to improve customer service.)

Another aspect of groups is membership. Who belongs to the group? Who does not? Who is present at the group's meetings and who is not? Who is accepted, and who is not? Group members sense the level of membership they have in the group. Activities that include everyone (as suggested in Step One) give everyone a chance to be equally involved. Teams that approach their work together with a desire to balance participation and include everyone have a better chance of keeping team members active and loyal to the group. Sometimes a team member will be uncomfortable with the concept of teams, or will not feel he or she is part of the group for some reason. The member may withdraw during meetings or miss team meetings altogether. When a group allows a member to withdraw or be absent, without making an effort to bring them back in, it loses cohesiveness. Over time, other members may conclude it's all right to drop out when they lose motivation or feel lack of acceptance. For example, some teams have allowed a number of members to leave by not attending team meetings. The rest of the members were never quite clear as to who was on the team and who was not. These teams lost the strength and stability needed for consensus. The more faithful members still felt they had to seek buy-in from the absent members when important decisions were made. This bogged down the teams and prevented them from performing at their best. Groups need to work actively to include their members, which means getting them to come to the meetings.

Another factor in group dynamics is the need to allow time for interaction and venting of tensions. Group process seems to demand time for tensions to be released and people to veer off the path of the discussion. If too tight controls are placed on the group for the sake of efficiency, if people are not allowed to wander from the topic, and if prolonged discussion of certain proposals is not allowed, the group can become tense, inhibited, and ultimately less productive and creative. What may look to an observer like gross inefficiency may indeed result in a higher quality of work. A skilled team facilitator and experienced team members know rather instinctively when it is better to let the group wander off, relieve tension, vent frustrations, reformulate proposals, and debate the merits of options—than to try to enforce strict controls. After a period of time, the team winds down, or looks to someone to get it back on track. Meandering, interaction, and venting are all essential and important parts of group process. If the team has set clear goals, is working through the steps outlined in this book, and has a strong desire to produce results, the side paths it occasionally takes will provide data, insights, or interaction the team needs to either do its work or become more cohesive as a team.

Recognize the Stages of Teamwork

When groups of people work together, they require time to develop into a productive unit. Some team members will openly express concern that more work is not getting completed in the early stages of teamwork. As mentioned earlier, this is natural.

In his work on group dynamics, Bruce Tuckman[1] observed that the work of groups typically proceeded through five common, predictable stages. He pointed out that groups do not usually produce or perform much until the fourth stage. It helps teams to understand that they are likely to experience these natural stages of teamwork. Tuckman labeled these stages as follows:

Forming—The stage when group members get to know one another and size up one another's role or influence in the group.

Storming—The stage when group members hold forth their individual ideas and opinions, disagreeing, and debating with one another. This stage finds teams struggling over purpose and goals, team members vying for leadership and influence, and getting organized.

Norming—The stage when group members have settled into working together, have established norms for working together, and begin to become cohesive as a group.

Performing—The stage when the group members have become a working unit and the group is producing results.

Adjourning—The stage when the group acknowledges its time as a unit is over, celebrates its achievements, and disbands.

In my work with teams, I have watched them go through these stages with a fair amount of predictability. Sometimes teams proceed straight through them, but usually as a team develops, it occasionally loops back to one of the earlier stages. Sometimes a team

---

[1]B. W. Tuckman, "Developmental Sequence in Small Groups." *Psychological Bulletin,* 1965, Vol. 63, pp. 384–399. Copyright © 1965 by the American Psychological Association. Reprinted with permission.

gets stuck in one stage, unable to move on. Such a team may need outside support, such as a skilled facilitator or experienced team to pull it through. Some teams get through all the stages faster than others, but seldom can a team skip one of the stages and be productive later.

I prefer to call the final stage of group development *transforming* instead of *adjourning*, because not all teams adjourn or disband; instead, some teams change focus or membership, transforming themselves in some way to start over as a team. Even high-performing groups generally wind down in some fashion after a period of performing. It is then that the transforming stage sets in. In the transforming stage, the team either disbands or renews itself. The completion of a team's work occurs somewhere between the performing and transforming stages.

Help the Team Move Through Each Stage

The team leader and team members play an important part in helping the team move through these stages successfully by contributing in different ways during each of the stages. The following chart illustrates how the team leader's and team members' roles change as the team develops. Team leaders and members contribute better to team efforts by understanding how important their roles are at each stage of the team's development. If your team is in the forming stage, for example, team members need to understand the initial tasks of the team and avoid cliques, which will divide the team. When your team is in the storming stage, members will need to speak up, show respect for diverse opinions, initiate ideas, build solutions from everyone's ideas, and help the team reach consensus. During the performing stage, team members will need to keep their commitments, complete action items, provide information and support to the team, and keep the team's goals in mind. This would not be a good time to suggest that the team is on the wrong track or that the team should take on extra goals.

The team leader's role evolves over the life of the team, from a more directive and boundary-setting role in the team's forming stage to a more consultative role during the performing stage. Throughout the entire life of the team, the leader plays more of a facilitative than a management role. When the team is in the transforming stage, the team leader plays a key role in helping the team understand whether it needs to disband or continue as a team.

Learning to recognize these stages of team development will help your team move from its infant (forming) stage, during which little real work gets done, to a mature (performing) stage, when the team's output is high.

It is generally impossible to skip a stage, because each stage of development is important. However, with awareness and practice, team members and leaders can adjust expectations and behave in ways that will move their team through each stage successfully, without bogging down or giving up.

Team members can review the team-development chart with their team and discuss the following questions:

- What stage are we in at this time? (Honor differences of opinion. Some members may disagree as to what stage the team is in. Ask them to explain their view.)

- Have we successfully completed prior stages? Why or why not?

- Do we need to loop back through any stage? Why or why not?

- What have we learned that will help us move ahead?

- What blocks and barriers are we facing in our team development?

- What progress have we made?

- What additional steps should we take to further our team's development?

TABLE 1 Stages of Team Development

	1. Forming	2. Storming	3. Norming	4. Performing	5. Transforming
Characteristics	Politeness Tentative joining Membership may be unstable Orienting personally and professionally Gathering impressions Avoiding controversy Hidden agendas Cliques may form Need for safety and approval	Struggles over purpose and goals Vying for leadership Differences in points of view and personal style become evident Lack of role clarity Reliance on voting, arbitration, leader-made decisions Team organizing itself and its work	Cohesion, harmony Balanced influence Open-minded Trust builds Comfortable with relationships Cliques dissolved Focus and energy on tasks Planning *how* to work as a team Confidence and creativity high	Team fully functional Roles clear Interdependent Team able to organize itself Flexible Members function well individually, in subgroups, or as a team Empathy for one another	Internal or external forces bring about *renewal, change, or dissolution* Momentum slows down Activities mark the ending or renewal of team efforts
Team Identity	Individual identity prevails	Individual identity still strong; team identity begins to build	Team identity emerges	Team identity strong	Team identity dissolves or renews
Leader's Role	*Visionary/Director* Provide structure and clear task direction Allow get-acquainted time Create atmosphere of confidence, optimism Active involvement	*Facilitator/Teacher* Acknowledge conflict Guide toward consensus Get members to assume more task responsibility Teach conflict resolution methods Offer support and praise Active involvement	*Coach/Sponsor* Give feedback and support Plan celebrations Allow for less structure Continue to focus on building strong relationships Less involvement	*Consultant/Sponsor* Give positive reinforcement and support Offer consultation Keep channels of communication open Share new information Allow team to organize itself and to test new procedures	*Facilitator/Visionary* Help team develop options for renewing or disbanding Guide the process Help team design its "rituals" for renewal or ending Offer sincere appreciation for team's accomplishments

Team Members' Role	Ask questions to get clear about team's initial tasks Avoid cliques Get to know each member Have patience with the process Listen Suspend judgment	Consider all views Initiate ideas Aim for synergy Help team reach consensus on goals, purpose, roles Build solutions from everyone's needs Accept conflict as natural Respect diversity of team members	Take responsibility to influence *how* team works Keep a realistic outlook Avoid harmony for sake of harmony Be flexible Support efforts to build "team spirit" Initiate and consider new ideas	Keep goals in mind Maintain flexibility Continue consensus process Complete action items Provide information to team Support and verify team norms Keep momentum going	Accept need for team to "move on" Participate fully in efforts to *end* or *renew* team Help evaluate team's success Carry forth learning to next team effort
Pitfalls (ways to get stuck in this stage)	Staying too polite Lack of clear direction	Lack of conflict resolution skills No one to facilitate conflict resolution Individuals stuck on own agendas "Turf wars" and "tree hugging"	"Groupthink" Comfort Focus too much on relationships, ignore tasks Unwilling to take risk External change which may alter team's purpose	"Burnout" Team not evaluating and/or correcting itself Lack of training OK to stay here if productive	Failing to renew when it's time Renewing too soon Unwilling to disband team when its work is done Not honoring the *process* of transforming
Bridge to next stage	Adequate comfort level	Collective "win"	Confidence, Risk-Taking	Reflection, Evaluation	A definite ending, change or renewal
Conflict	Low	High	Low	Healthy Conflict (Team has learned ways to resolve differences)	Low
Output	Low	Low	Low—Medium	High	Temporarily tapers off or ends

Source: Based on Bruce Tuckman's classifications of the stages of group development (1965). Tuckman's 5th stage is called "Adjourning." © 1997 Rees & Associates. From "Developmental Sequence in Small Groups," by D. W. Tuckman. *Psychological Bulletin,* Vol. 63, pp. 384–399. Used by permission.

Celebrating Team Milestones

Healthy teams learn to work hard and then to celebrate when they have completed an important milestone. In a recent book, *From Beginning to End*, about the rituals of our lives, Robert Fulghum advises us to celebrate important milestones in our lives. This advice is also important for teams:

> It never makes sense to wait until your life is in a perfect state of grace to celebrate its joys and passages. Never hesitate to celebrate.[1]

A team can lose momentum if it fails to stop from time to time and recognize its achievements. Sometimes team accomplishments are glazed over, and team members move on to the next task without reviewing what has already been done successfully. The team needs to practice saying, "Look what we have achieved so far!" Each team will have its own major milestones that will have to be defined by the team. Depending on the scope of your team's work and the time the team is together, the members will want to mark progress with some type of celebration or recognition.

The team can easily recognize its accomplishments during a meeting. The team may want to design a chart to post in the team

[1]Robert Fulghum, *From Beginning to End* (New York: Villard, 1995).

meeting room which shows the milestone completed in one column, date completed in another column, obstacles overcome in the next column, and celebration planned in the final column. If it is unrealistic for the team to celebrate every milestone, the team can celebrate several milestones at once.

What to Celebrate or Recognize

The team will ultimately have to define what its own major milestones are and whether to simply recognize the progress or to have a celebration. Sometimes the team will want to recognize or celebrate overcoming a major obstacle. Following are some suggestions as to what the team may wish to celebrate:

- Completing the team charter (Step One)
- Completing the first major action item in the actual work of the team (during Step Five)
- Major milestones in the work of the team (These can be identified during the writing of the charter [Step One] or during the planning stage [Step Four].)
- Any difficult decision reached by consensus
- Any significant improvement in the way the team functions, based on efforts made after the team has done a self-evaluation (Step Seven)
- Accomplishment of the team's mission or goals (Successful completion of the Team Charter)

Ways to Celebrate or Recognize

The way the team celebrates and rewards itself will, of course, depend on the team's resources and desires. This can be difficult to decide because of the diversity of the team members. For example, some may find an after work pizza party a great way to celebrate team achievement; others may find this an inconvenience in their lives. Celebrations do not have to occur after work hours (i.e., during people's leisure time). Time can be taken after a meeting, during lunch, or even during a meeting to celebrate the team's success. The team should try to balance out the needs of its members and celebrate in ways that will please everyone over time. The team could make some celebrations optional.

The goal of celebrating is to provide an opportunity for the team to reward itself while recognizing its successes. The benefits of adequate team recognition are many: The team takes time out to recognize its own achievement, which builds team confidence and pride. The team gets a chance to rest and regain momentum after it has completed some hard work. Team members get a chance to build trust and rapport with one another by spending non-work, social time together.

An issue that frequently comes up in teamwork is should individuals on the team be recognized or must the whole team always be recognized? In general, it is the whole team that needs to be recognized. However, there are times when individuals have made important contributions to a team effort, and it would be a mistake not to recognize them. The best way to do this is to have the team members themselves say something about the effort. Allow every team member to comment on the team's recent success. The team leader or the facilitator can use some open questions to stimulate their thinking, for example:

- What was particularly significant about our recent achievement?
- What did we do well that we want to repeat again?
- What obstacles did we overcome? How?
- What did we learn? (Do not concentrate on the negative, after all, it is a celebration/recognition!)
- Who on our team would you like to thank for their special effort?
- What was humorous about our achievement or efforts?

Some of the ways teams mark their milestones and celebrate their successes are as follows:

- Have a pizza party or other refreshments at the workplace.
- Call a short meeting just to recognize the achievement.
- Have a social event after work, such as a barbecue at a team member's house, a picnic, dinner or lunch at a restaurant, attending a sport or cultural event, and so on.
- Keep a chart in the team meeting room and mark progress with colorful stars, stickers, or other creative methods.
- Give "comp-time certificates," which allow team members to take time off work to help compensate for extra hours put in.
- Have T-shirts made for the team (the team members can choose the design).
- Give a memento, such as ballpoint pens, notebooks, or coffee mugs, to recognize the team.
- Provide the team with a cake, ice cream, maybe something healthy, such as fruit, nuts, raisins, and popcorn. Let the team decide.

Fostering Team Creativity

Creativity is a key aspect of teamwork. Activities such as brainstorming, gathering information, finding resources, making decisions, coming up with solutions, or designing programs or processes—all require creativity.

There is usually some mystique associated with creativity. Many people believe that creativity is either inherited or that it is some kind of special gift bestowed only upon certain individuals. While *creative geniuses*, people who produce copious amounts of innovative work in their lifetimes, may not ever be common, we know today that all people have creative potential and that creativity skills and habits can be taught and learned.

Creativity can be defined as "the ability to generate new and useful ideas."[1] A common misconception is that creativity is only the act of coming up with ideas; however, creativity includes sorting and selecting out the most useful ideas. Creativity is, in fact, an entire process of conceiving a desired end result through selecting the best idea and implementing it.

The problem is no longer how to generate enough new and useful ideas, but rather how to sort and select from all the

---

[1]E. Glassman, *The Creativity Factor: Unlocking the Potential of Your Team* (San Francisco: Pfeiffer, 1991). Copyright ©1991 by Pfeiffer, an imprint of Jossey-Bass Publishers.

ideas generated. . . . Creativity is needed to solve problems throughout the entire process of innovation. We need to realize that on-the-job creativity and creative thinking are daily, ongoing processes of transforming old ideas into new and that creativity procedures are important in all steps in the innovation process.[2]

The Creative Process

Creativity flows in stages and each stage is necessary. Rushing the process does not work. When your team is facing a problem that it must solve, a decision to make, or a new process to design, it should try to work within the natural process of creativity. There are definite stages in the creative process:

Conception This is a general idea of what the team wants the end result to be. Just what is it the team wants to create? What does it want to bring into being that is not there now? (If the team is facing a problem, do not focus on the problem. Focus on what it will be like when the problem is not there.) The team should know where it wants to go.

Groundwork The team members should prepare themselves for the work. Gather facts, do research, brainstorm ideas, follow hunches. Look at the reality of the current situation in relation to the results the team wants. What is the gap there?

Action and Application The team members should apply themselves to the creation. Clarify what it is the team is creating and focus on that. Take action to bring the creation into being. Make choices and experiment to come closer and closer to the team's desired end result. Concentrate totally on inventing a solution.

[2]Glassman, *The Creativity Factor*.

Evaluation and Adjustment The team will learn that some things work and some do not. Members should learn from their actions and adjust their creative work accordingly. Keep choosing and trying, evaluating and adjusting.

Incubation Take time out. Most creative pursuits require time away from the problem before the solution presents itself. Seek distractions from the work. Work on other things. Do not touch the creative work for a while. The team will come back to the problem refreshed.

Solution After incubation, the solution frequently appears effortlessly. The team may suddenly find a solution because of its earlier diligence and focused desire. Some of the best ideas seem to pop out while you are not looking for them (e.g., while driving, showering, dreaming, watching an unrelated movie, chatting with a friend). Teams will also experience this phenomenon of creativity, the moment of "Aha!" when illumination occurs.

Implementation The creative effort is not finished until the idea has been successfully implemented, until the idea has proven itself useful. It requires discipline and action to bring the idea into effect, to make it the new reality. This stage requires polishing, adding final touches, and finally bringing the creative process to an end—declaring it complete. Sometimes one piece of creative work spurs on other creations. It is important to know when the work is complete, to declare the work done, and then, if desired, move on to the next creation.

When teams learn about this process of creativity, they understand better why certain team procedures really work. They are patterned after the creative process.

How to Spark Team Creativity

There are habits the team can learn that will jump-start its creativity. Reviewing these from time to time, especially before beginning a creative piece of work, will help team members foster, not stifle, creativity.

- Commit to considering every idea, as opposed to automatically discarding it. Try to find some merit in every idea.
- Practice responding to every idea with interest and curiosity, instead of criticism.
- Try to find both positive and negative aspects to every idea. The positive aspects become assets and the negative aspects represent handicaps to overcome.
- Learn to say, "This idea could work if. . . ." This will stop you from responding with an automatic "No, it won't work because. . . ."
- Postpone evaluation and judgment of new ideas until they have been clarified, discussed, and considered.
- Learn to state what you like about the idea first.
- Avoid jumping to an early conclusion.
- Be patient with the creative process.
- Accept the fact that there are times when you will feel lost or confused. This is part of the creative process.
- Allow spontaneity and humor; they help the creative process.

Do not stifle creativity by saying things like, "We've never done it that way before," or "It won't work here," or "We tried that, and it didn't work," or "Management will never go for it." One way the team can learn to think creatively about ideas is to divide the group into two sub-groups. The facilitator or the team leader should ask each sub-group to list positive aspects of an idea that received an early rejection. Have each sub-group work quickly and come up with as many positive qualities as it can. Reward the sub-group that comes up with the most positive comments.

If the team has a lot of creative work to do, or one important creative project, it should take time to assess its creativity potential and determine changes it should implement. An excellent tool for such an assessment is a book titled *The Creativity Factor: Unlocking the Potential of Your Team* by Edward Glassman.[3] This book offers many ideas and methods to enhance creativity in a team. The facilitator or the team leader should have the team use Appendix F of Glassman's book, "A Questionnaire to Assess Your Team's Creativity Potential," to assess the team's creativity potential. After each team member has taken and scored the questionnaire, the facilitator should record each member's total for each section (A through G) on a flip chart. Then, as a team, have the team review the scores and answer the following questions:

- Where do we need to improve?
- Where are we doing well?
- Where are there discrepancies between our individual scores? Why?
- What steps should we take to increase our team's creativity potential?

[3]Glassman, *The Creativity Factor*.

APPENDIX

Team Member Credo

Teamwork is simply you and I working well together to achieve a common purpose. As a team member, I acknowledge and value the unique needs and creative abilities of each fellow team member, yet I understand that, through synergy, we can be stronger and more effective as a unit.

I understand that it is my role to work continually on the two important aspects of teamwork: (1) getting the job done and (2) relating well to one another.

I understand that the transition to a "team culture" means that my role is changing, your role is changing, and the roles of our managers are changing. I will strive to be patient with myself and others in this transition.

I understand that to perform well as a team member, I must learn new skills and take risks to express my ideas and try new approaches. I understand that it is also my role to listen and carefully consider the ideas of others and to support them when they take risks. When others do a good job or go out of their way to help me or the team, I will remember to say "Thank you."

When problems or misunderstandings occur between me and my teammates, I will try to be direct and non-critical to solve our problems. I commit to resolving conflicts without resorting to the use of power or authority, or to win at the expense of the other's losing. I respect your needs, but I must also respect my own.

I will not think of our team as "an island unto itself," but will find opportunities to link up with those outside the team to gain support, knowledge, and understanding. I acknowledge that effective teams value the opinions and needs of their customers, suppliers, managers, and members of the larger organization. I will encourage my team to reach out and learn from others who have been there before us or who are struggling as we are.

And, finally, I understand that successful performance as a team is not a stop or an event, but a *process*, a continual evolution of awareness and growth. Teams move forward in stages, and progress is not always even. Throughout the process of our team's development, I will keep the destination foremost in mind: working together in mutual respect for continually improved performance.

READINGS/RESOURCES

Daniels, William R. (1986). *Group power: A manager's guide to using meetings*. San Francisco: Pfeiffer.

Fisher, Aubrey. (1980). *From beginning to end*. New York: Villard.

Fisher, Kimball, Steven Rayner, William Belgard, and the Belgard, Fisher, Rayner team. (1995). *Tips for teams*. New York: McGraw Hill. See "Goal Setting and Measuring Results" to get help in setting team goals.

Glassman, Edward (1991). *The creativity factor: Unlocking the potential of your team*. San Francisco: Pfeiffer.

Harper, Bob and Ann Harper. (1991). *Succeeding as a self-directed work team*. New York: MW Corporation.

Katzenbach, Jon and Douglas Smith. (1993). *The wisdom of teams*. New York: Harper Collins.

Kinlaw, Dennis, C. (1993). *Team-managed facilitation: Critical skills for developing self-sufficient teams*. San Francisco: Pfeiffer.

Quinlivan-Hall, David and Peter Renner. (1990). *In search of solutions*. Vancouver: PFR Training Associates. See "The Problem Solving Process" for help in approaching and solving problems as a team.

Rees, Fran (1991). *How to lead work teams: Facilitation skills*. San Francisco: Pfeiffer.

Saint, Steven and James R. Lawson. (1994). *Rules for reaching consensus*. San Francisco: Pfeiffer.

Schein, Edgar (1980). *Organizational psychology*. New York: Prentice-Hall.

Scholtes, Peter R. (1988). *The team handbook*. Madison, WI: Joiner Associates. This book gives excellent guidance to project teams. See

"Five-Stage Plan for Process Improvement" if your team needs a method for how to go about improving a process.

Shonk, James H. (1992). *Team-based organizations*. Homewood, Illinois: Business One Irwin.

Spiegel, Jerry and Cresencio Torres. (1994). *Manager's official guide to team working*. San Francisco: Pfeiffer. This book also contains help in team problem solving (see "Problem Solving").

Tagliere, Daniel A. (1993). *How to meet, think and work to consensus*. San Francisco: Pfeiffer. See "The Creative Problem Solving Procedure" for help in creative problem solving in teams. "The Planning/Project Management Procedure" will give your team tips in planning a team project. "The Presentation Planning Procedure" will help plan a team presentation.

Tague, Nancy R. (1995). *The quality toolbox*. Milwaukee, WI: ASQC Quality Press. Many group methods are explained that will help your team organize data, solve problems, make decisions, and improve a process.

Weisbord, Marvin (1987). *Productive workplaces: Organizing and managing for dignity, meaning, and community*. San Francisco: Jossey-Bass.

Index

Advanced training designs prepare teams for future responsibilities

Team Building for the Future
Beyond the Basics

Robin L. Elledge & Steven L. Phillips

This comprehensive, team-building resource provides you with the right information and training designs to help you tackle specific issues or overcome difficulties that today's teams face.

These training designs help you intervene effectively with:

- **Trustless** teams
- **Teams** in chaos
- **Temporary** task teams
- **Merged** teams . . . and more!

The customizable training designs are complete with activities, objectives, guidelines, handout and flip chart content, and overhead masters. This resource also introduces a new model of team effectiveness and is most useful if you already have fundamental group-process and team-building skills.

Objective:	Each module addresses the needs in a specific type of team and each activity outlines its specific objective.
Timing:	Varies with each module—each can be customized. Activities vary in time from 15 minutes to 3 hours.
Audience:	All levels of employees in a team.

The all-in-one resource to execute team-building programs

The Team-Building Source Book

Steven L. Phillips & Robin L. Elledge

Here is everything you need to lead a group through team building! You can help a group accomplish specific, basic tasks necessary for productive work. Plus, you can adapt each module as needed to meet your groups' unique circumstances.

This handy, looseleaf volume gives you instructions, reproducible handouts, information for flip charts, samples of assessment materials, and complete coverage of the team-building process! Includes 11 complete interventions that address basic team needs such as: • Clarifying roles • Conflict management • Problem solving • And more.

Each section covers a different phase:

- Getting Started
- The Data-Collection Process
- Analyzing the Data
- Giving Feedback
- Implementation
- Follow-Up

Objective:	Introduce the facilitator to the basics of team building.
Timing:	Varies with each module— from 1 to 4 hours.
Audience:	All levels of employees in a team.

Improve group results as a successful leader-facilitator

How to Lead Work Teams

Facilitation Skills

Fran Rees

Now you can reap the benefits of a more facilitative, participative style of leadership! *How to Lead Work Teams* will help you increase cooperation and job satisfaction, raise productivity and quality levels, and gain a more favorable view of your leadership abilities through facilitation. It describes exactly what facilitation is and what it is not and how to do it effectively.

It shows you how to:

- **Involve** others, build consensus, and get commitment
- **Help** others solve problems and make decisions
- **Use** the knowledge and experience of all employees
- **Develop** and lead a team
- **Use** group process to run effective team meetings

This book is especially helpful for someone who is new to managing or leading a team. It will also help experienced team leaders refine the role of "leader-facilitator." And it will help team members understand how facilitation works and how they can enhance the process.

Now anyone can develop and lead a successful team with these experiential activities!

25 Activities for Teams

25 Activities for Teams is a useful collection of activities and assessment tools for leading and developing high-performing work teams. Designed to complement the popular *How to Lead Work Teams*, this resource can also stand alone to help team leaders get everyone actively involved in the team's development.

Reinforcing Fran Rees' LEAD model, the activities in this book will help the team leader:

- **Lead** with a clear purpose
- **Empower** participants
- **Aim** for consensus
- **Direct** the process

25 Activities for Teams is a valuable resource that promotes fun, experiential, team learning. Best of all, it can be used by even novice team leaders and facilitators or by professional trainers. This collection brings together exercises from a variety of resources that will help teams develop skills, build cohesiveness, and accomplish important tasks.

CALL FREE: 800.274.4434

FAX FREE: 800.569.0443